What?!
You Don't Want Children?
Understanding Rejection
in the Childfree Lifestyle

What?!
You Don't Want Children?
Marcia Drut-Davis

atmosphere press

Table of Contents

Author's Note...3

Foreword, by Dr. Duffy Spencer 5

Introduction...13

Chapter 1:
Rejection by Family and Friends 17

Chapter 2:
Pronatalism...39

Chapter 3:
Promises Not Kept 59

Chapter 4:
Rejection While Traveling..71

Chapter 5:
Rejection in the Workplace 85

Chapter 6:
Military Stories...103

Chapter 7:
The NotMom Summit 123

Chapter 8:
Childfree Men..135

Chapter 9:
Facing Rejection Worldwide..149

Chapter 10:
Rejection from Within 191

Chapter 11:
Rejection: A Tale of Acceptance, by Sam Nugent...........205

Chapter 12:
Rejecting Cancer 219

Chapter 13:
Eliminating Rejection: Is it possible?.............................229

Acknowledgements 243

Author's Note

This book is birthed to help readers face and overcome rejection in the childfree lifestyle. It reflects the author's recollections of experiences over time. Some names and personal characteristics of people who were interviewed, or who shared with the author via messaging, phone, FaceTime, Skype, Instagram, Twitter, and many childfree support sites on Facebook, have been changed to protect their privacy. Some events have been compressed, and some dialogue has been recreated.

Foreword

Duffy Spencer, PhD, social psychologist, and licensed mental health counselor, conducted her doctoral research on Women and Deviance. As a college professor, she taught Sociology of the Family, Social Problems, and Group Dynamics, among others. Currently Dr. Spencer has a clinical practice treating individuals and couples in Westbury, New York.

A keynote speaker on the topic of "Living Your Life Your Way," Dr. Spencer is the author of *SPICE: the Essential Ingredients for Effective Living* and the *Relationship Doctor* CD series, and co-author of *Dealing with Difficult People* and *Leadership Strategists*.

Known as the Relationship Doctor™, "Dr. Duffy" is the host of the WHPC (90.3 FM) radio show *Just Relationships*. She also teaches "Self-Esteem Building" and "Winning Relationships" courses at Nassau Community College and hosts retreats for "Women in Transition."

*****

So you decided to do your own thing: be unconventional and not have children. You want to be a free agent and live your own life, either as a single woman or in a committed relationship. If people hear you're choosing the childfree lifestyle, you start getting flak—and disapproval. They don't like your choice, or they don't like you—or both! It's a personal choice, isn't it? It's not supposed to hurt, but it does.

I've helped many clients who face societal expectations and then feel socially rejected. When their actions are perceived as defiant and intentional, as is often the case in choosing a childfree lifestyle, personal attacks, unfair treatment, and harassment often follow. It can be a shock, and it can seem unfair. People who're brave enough to ask for help defending against pronatalistic finger-pointing want to find ways to cope with such harsh condemnations.

We live in a pronatal society where parenthood is idealized. It's no surprise, then, that many people are sorely disillusioned upon becoming parents. They may even experience an underlying and unnamed sense of being "conned." They were promised the sugar-coated stories that accompany parenting, but found many of those stories to be just myths. It's one thing to be okay with following implicit rules so long as everyone else does. It's another thing when someone goes against the very same rules one has so assiduously followed and that seems to be okay. It is infuriating and highly uncomfortable for those who choose not to have children to be negatively judged.

After forty years of living the childfree lifestyle, Marcia Drut-Davis knew she was onto something when she began receiving constant inquiries on her blog, Facebook support sites, and Instagram from readers of her memoir. The most common question was about how to overcome the feelings of rejection and even shame that accompany such a personal choice. To make matters worse, we can even feel ashamed about feeling ashamed!

Since knowledge is power, understanding why rejection is so painful can free us from the shame of experiencing it.

Whenever you face rejection, examine these important questions:

* Why is the fear of rejection such a powerful

demotivator?

* Why do people reject each other?

* How can we live a happy life of quality despite rejection?

Humans are hardwired to fear rejection. Why? It's very simple. If one is rejected by the group, they die. Throughout millennia, individuals who couldn't carry their own weight because of age or infirmity were simply left behind. With limited resources, people couldn't sustain care for people faced with such disadvantages.

The young need others for their physical survival. The human infant takes a long time to mature, so modern humans are vulnerable and dependent for decades. As social animals, interaction with others forms our sense of identity. Being naturally dependent upon others, we have an inherent need to belong, and we want to be accepted members of the human group.

Yet any kind of difference can seem threatening. If a baby chick is dyed pink, it's pecked to death. Whether it's a difference in appearance, stamina, gender, behavior, or life choice, group members who go against the norm are at risk of being ostracized.

In some societies, as you'll read in the chapter about international rejection, people who deviate from group norms are stoned to death, or ignored to death. Which is worse? People die psychologically—they lose their identity—when they are not seen. Invisible, they fail to exist emotionally, and eventually they physically die. Even in modern times, when individuals can pay for goods and services and afford to live alone, they still need a sense of belonging with others.

One would think differences would be acceptable in

such a diverse society as ours. Yet who among us has not experienced the pain of rejection from being different? Whether it's a matter of height, weight, hair, braces, glasses, sports performance, skin color, religion, or nonconformity, no one escapes.

The question becomes: "Am I willing to give up myself to avoid rejection?" Marcia Drut-Davis gave a resounding "No." I don't imagine you would want to, either. Yet, it's very important to note that having the wherewithal to consciously choose an alternative lifestyle doesn't exempt you from the pain of being shunned.

As we claim the right to be childfree, we claim the right to experience the pain that may come from being ridiculed, reprimanded, fired, gossiped about, and the like. As social beings, we still want to be "part of" and to feel welcome. Ideally, we want it on our own terms. Yet marching to the tune of a different drummer is not for the faint of heart. Though we stand by our choice, we can be plagued by difficult feelings and thoughts. This requires an honest self-reckoning with such questions as:

1. "Who am I?"
2. "Who do I want to be?"
3. "Who do I want to be with?"

If you're reading this book, you're looking to find your own way with your grace and dignity intact. Or maybe you're reading this book to raise your own consciousness. Perhaps you have a son or daughter who doesn't want children, and that in turn has made you feel rejected. It takes courage to experience painful feelings head-on. It can mean encountering any number of emotional triggers. We may even have to face the residual childhood fear of not pleasing others. While such challenges face both genders, females are particularly vulnerable to the need to people-please. If we are not willing to live a counterfeit life, how can we reconcile our choices with our need to belong? We are challenged to go on an inner journey of self-discovery.

People are complicated and have a multitude of thoughts, needs, and feelings. In a world characterized by changing values, it's not unusual to have inner conflicts. Therefore, it's important not to judge ourselves. Self-acceptance is the key to inner peace. All we can be is what we are in any given moment. "This is what it's *really* like for me" is the necessary self-statement. We want emotional connection, and we have the right to ask ourselves: with whom, and on what terms? When we answer these questions, we can make choices based on self-knowledge and self-discernment. In giving ourselves permission to experience conflicting needs and values, we build healthy defenses against the vitriol of others. Understanding where we stand in the midst of societal change offers us a more objective and grounded perspective.

For instance, it's only in recent times that birth control is a viable possibility. Only one hundred years ago, Margaret Sanger was jailed for even suggesting a woman could control how many children to have.

There are other factors to consider as well. The structure of the American economy has changed. Now, rather than children being another set of farmhands, they're a financial liability. Also, there is no longer a need for everyone to propagate the species in an already overpopulated world. Though such changes have shifted societal norms, the notion of a fertile woman choosing to forgo motherhood is still heretical to some. Even the idea can evoke feelings of indignation ("You mean you have a choice and I didn't?"), anger ("How dare you not take the responsibility I have to bear?"), or even grief in people facing infertility ("How can you choose against something I would give anything to have?"). Such reactions are subjective and unconscious. Understanding the pain behind such reactions enables us to not take them so personally.

As we gain clarity about our own motivations and needs, we free ourselves from self-rejection. We may find some of our needs conflicting and feel torn in different directions. We may, from time to time, depending on circumstances, feel the ancient pull of the mother-child or father-child bond, yet still choose not to have children. We simply acknowledge that we have unconsciously internalized societal "shoulds." For instance, women shouldn't practice self-care less they be labeled selfish. A lifetime of socialization to be pleasing induces guilt: "I'm wrong to take care of myself and not children." Another pull may be a sense of missing out on membership in the "Parent Club."

By feeling our feelings, we move through them and they ease. The Latin roots of the word "emotion" are *e* (out) and *movere* (move)—to move out. This is actually a countercultural act in a world suspicious of feelings. Yet, we can choose whether to follow cultural dictates against emotional expression. To heal the pain of rejection, we're challenged to feel that pain and to bring unresolved hurts into conscious awareness.

As we face any inner conflicts honestly, we find those conflicts overruled by our desire to live life on our own terms. As we accept residual yearnings, we become free to accept the joys of childfree living.

Marcia's illustration of the upsides of a childfree life helps to level the playing field for true choice. If all possible choices are deemed valid, we're free to admire the parenting of others and the gift of children for those who are so inclined. Choices do not have to be all good or all bad, or one side versus the other. It's human to experience ambivalence, a sense of loss, and a sense of gain. If one feels sadness or loss with either choice, that feeling can simply be felt. It need not imply regret for the choice we've made. Living according to our own sense of self ultimately leads to our happiness and fulfillment.

In a world where the goal is self-development for all, each person is emboldened to fulfill their own unique happiness. That is why Marcia Drut-Davis' book is so important. She explores, in depth, many experiences of facing rejection in the childfree lifestyle. It will validate your own concerns and may even provide an "aha" explanation for other experiences you hadn't been aware of.

Her brilliant treatise on the benefits of childfree living sheds light on our own path to self-actualization. By raising your consciousness about the often-felt and rarely discussed rejections that arise while traveling, in the workplace, in pronatalistic advertising and movies, in the military, in the eyes of men, within the movement itself, even in the prospect of a terminal disease, you'll feel acknowledged and accepted. You'll think about Marcia asking if we can ever bridge the gap that divides child-freedom from parenting and lauds parenting as righteous. You'll enjoy reading her suggestions for remedying rejection. You will find clarity about the difference between childfree and childless, as she learned as the keynote speaker at the 2017 NotMom Summit. In more than one chapter, you'll identify with what Marcia shares. If not, you'll at least learn compassion.

Finally, in the words of Howard Thurman, an African-American author, philosopher, theologian, educator, and civil rights leader: "Don't ask yourself what the world needs. Ask what makes you come alive, and go do it."

What the world needs is people who have come alive. Ultimately, there is no "other." There is just "us." There is just "you." I wish you an exciting journey of coming fully alive and enjoying your childfree life.

Introduction

Dear Readers:

I'm your author, Marcia Drut-Davis. I wrote *Confessions of a Childfree Woman* in 2013. It was a personal catharsis to share the journey I experienced after "coming out" as a childfree woman on the acclaimed documentary TV show *60 Minutes*. The book also explores whether there were any regrets associated with choosing that lifestyle, and what happened after that TV exposure. Losing my job as a teacher and facing death threats (though my then-husband received none) was frightening. Being a guest speaker escorted by police past picket lines with signs saying "Godless Bitch" stunned me. Being shunned by family and friends was my shocking baptism into the negative effects of pronatalism.

After the book was published, I was diagnosed with cancer. This shook me to my core. During months of chemo and radiation, I thought, "Okay, if this is my end, what's left to do before I die?" I wrote a personal bucket list: more traveling, quality experiences with friends and family I love, exercise, better eating habits, and taking Latin dance lessons. I also questioned whether I did enough to support the childfree lifestyle. Once I finished the grueling fight and saw that I not only survived, but indeed seemed to thrive, I reconnected with my first book editor, Justine Duhr.

I told her, "I think I should update my book. I left out too much!" She wisely answered, "Okay, make a list of what you think you missed and let's talk!" Then, in her wonderfully intuitive way, she said, "You know, this could be another book."

13

So, here you are, reading that second book.

In my opinion, the one topic that my first book fails to address with enough depth and detail is facing rejection in the childfree lifestyle. This seems to be a challenge that too many people face worldwide.

My goals here are simple: I want to assure you that you're not alone in facing rejection over a personal lifestyle choice. Then, I want this book to either help you overcome that rejection, or help you live with it in a positive way.

There may be times throughout this book you're confused about my marital history. My first marriage was mentally abusive and ended after two years. We were married too young. My second marriage ended when my husband confessed his love for my then-girlfriend. They married and never had children. My third marriage, to Jim, my rock, is the keeper! No failures, only lessons.

If you're reading this book to gather more information and openly acknowledge that you may be guilty of rejecting someone, I think you're special. I want to inspire you to accept people's personal lifestyle choices even if you feel they're wrong. Acceptance trumps rejection. Pure love is unconditional. It also feels good to both the giver and the recipient.

Throughout this book, you'll find a lot of interviews and comments drawn from my open and closed childfree-support Facebook pages, my blog, Instagram, Twitter, and Reddit. For those who never go to Facebook, an open page is one that anyone can join. It's not as safe or private as a closed page, where people are vetted by administrators and moderators who try to keep out "trolls," who are usually critics of the childfree lifestyle, religious zealots, or parents who may feel we're personally attacking their children.

Authors write for many reasons. Some write to ignite their creative passions in the genre of fiction. Who hasn't connected with the human emotion conveyed by a well-crafted novel? I, however, write to support those of you who, for whatever reason, chose not to birth or raise children of your own. I write to support. I write to educate. I write to help others see the pain and rejection that too many people experience as a result of their personal choice!

I want you to walk this path with all the pride and dignity that any parent deserves. Keep this torch burning until we can put out the light, knowing it's an accepted and respected path to remain childfree by choice.

You're all loved.

Marcia

Chapter 1
Rejection by Family and Friends

"It's not love that hurts. What hurts is being hurt by someone you love."
—author unknown

"If you don't like something, change it. If you can't change it, change your attitude."
—Maya Angelou

One of the many challenges and heartbreaks childfree people may face is rejection by close family members or friends. Isn't blood supposed to be thicker than water? Families should be there for each other no matter what. They're supposed to stay together through the good, the bad, and the ugly, offering a haven in a storm and forgiveness when it's needed. Aren't authentic friendships the key to enjoying life?

It doesn't always work that way.

This chapter isn't meant to condemn the family or friends I've lost. It's to show that if you're experiencing similar trouble, you're not alone. I wish the family and friends who rejected me all the love, good health, and happiness in the world, and some healing for their upset hearts. I'm at peace having moved on.

****

"I need some time away from you," my sister, Rachel, texted me. "I don't know who you are now. I'm wondering if you were this way all my life and I never saw it."

I went numb. My hands tingled. It was hard to draw a breath, and my heart was pumping harder and faster. I felt a pain in the middle of my chest. *Oh, shit*, I thought. *Here it is.*

At seventy-two, with a family history full of heart disease, I assumed I was having a heart attack. My grandmother died at fifty-two from heart illness. My mother died at seventy-five after a quadruple bypass and valve replacement. Her surgery was a success, but her body betrayed her. She died of cardiogenic shock.

I sat down and tried to achieve a Zen-like focus on my breathing, drawing air slowly in while counting to six, holding for another six count, and letting it out even slower. I repeated that a few times until I felt the tingling dissipate. When I felt certain I wasn't having a heart attack, I looked back at the phone in my shaking hand.

My baby sister was telling me goodbye.

Or at least that's how it felt at the time. Sure, "I need some time away" isn't the same as "I need a lifetime away," but the text struck me as the beginning of the end of our relationship. Nearly sixty years into our sisterhood, we were having our first real fight.

We are half-sisters. Throughout our childhood and into adulthood we worked twice as hard at the relationship. It paid off. Neither of us were half of anything. We became not only the spiritual equivalent of full sisters, but best friends as well. We traveled to South America and along the blue Danube on a riverboat cruise. Everyone on that cruise called Rachel "Baby" because I kept saying she was my baby sister.

But after I published my memoir, I began to sense a slight shift in Rachel's approach toward me. Over time, that slight shift became more pronounced.

Three years later: "I need some time away from you."

Earlier that night we had gathered for a family dinner at Rachel's house. Her husband, Ben, was and still is a talented, much sought-after designer of estate homes. My eyes took in the details of their own lovely home: the beveled ceilings, the genuine marble floors, the floor-to-ceiling windows with drapes a rich blue to match their exquisite and expensive furniture.

The dining room table was huge, with a lovely tablecloth, china, and silver cutlery placed beside each napkin. The food was aromatic: bubbling brisket and gravy, steamed carrots, mashed potatoes, applesauce, broccoli, hot rolls, and several opened wine bottles. We were prepared for a fabulous family dinner.

Except it wasn't really my family. These were Ben's people, Rachel's in-laws. They always made an effort to include my husband, Jim, and me and make us feel warm and welcomed. Still, we were the outsiders.

I watched the other family members in animated conversation and envied their closeness. Whereas Rachel and I had very little family left, and none nearby, Ben came from a large family. Many of them lived very close, including his three sisters and their husbands. Ann and John lived only a few houses away. Gail and Evan were ten minutes away. Jackie and Ron had recently moved back to Florida from California to be closer to the family.

All their children were adults now, on their own and doing well after growing up together as cousins and best friends. The family was tightly knit through and through.

That night, Rachel sat next to me near the door so we could run in and out of the kitchen as needed. Nearby, at the head of the table, were my niece Fran and nephew Jordan sharing a long, mahogany piano bench.

Fran was in her mid-twenties, still unsure of what she wanted in a career. She was busy discussing this with one of her uncles, telling him about her disappointment with a job he had recently helped her find.

Jordan was on Fran's right, deep in conversation with his aunt Jackie about his experiences free-diving to spear large ocean fish. Jordan is passionate about deep-sea diving. He doesn't use oxygen tanks. Over the years he developed his lungs for free-diving. He lives for the joys of spearing large fish like tuna and grouper.

My husband, Jim, sat on my other side. Ben was at the other head of the table, opposite Fran and Jordan, and in front of the window, which was open to let in the balmy evening breeze.

One of Rachel's sisters-in-law asked if anyone had read her son's recently self-published book of poetry. Several family members responded with "Awesome," "Terrific," "So proud of him."

Nobody had mentioned this book's existence to me. Here I was, an honorary family member at least, not to mention an author, and yet none of them, Rachel included, had thought to tell me my sister's nephew published a book.

I felt alienated. I wondered if any of them, besides Rachel, even knew about my book. I asked for the title of the poetry book and commented how wonderful it was that he'd published it. Then I asked if anyone had read my memoir.

That's when the trouble began.

One of Rachel's brothers-in-law, Evan, already tipsy,

reaching for yet another sip of his wine, barked, "Why would any of us want to read your book? Isn't it about not wanting kids?"

I sat back and quietly replied, "Well, I thought you'd want to know how my life was affected by that choice. I see I'm mistaken."

The brother-in-law snidely replied, "Yup! None of us want to read it. We have kids and we love 'em."

Then Fran, my niece, chimed in: "Aunt Marcia, seriously?" she said, her eyes widening as if I'd just said something too ridiculous to comprehend. "My friends know about choices in having or not having kids. Everyone does! They don't need to read any book on *that* topic. Besides, I don't agree. That's why I never posted anything about your book on Facebook."

Everyone at the table stared at me, awaiting my reaction. I wanted to dig a hole through those gorgeous marble floors and crawl into it. I was embarrassed, and hurt. I could feel my face turning bright red.

I counted to ten to keep from lashing out. Jim squeezed my hand under the table. Jim is my third husband. (Don't judge me.) The two before him were lessons in everything I never wanted to experience again. They taught me the joy of having Jim in my life. Jim is a loving, supportive, funny, and fiercely protective husband. His twinkling green eyes, now-graying hair, and slight dimples are eye candy to me. But at that moment all I got was a squeezed hand.

Because of the connection I had with my sister and Jim, I expected them to come to my defense. Neither of them said a word. I made eye contact with Rachel, silently pleading, and finally, after much hesitation, she spoke up on my behalf.

Actually, she didn't. That is wishful thinking as I recall the event. What she said was, "Who wants coffee or tea with dessert?" Jim remained quiet, pushing some food around his plate. The topic of my memoir was gone like a bird taking flight.

It would be an understatement to say I was shocked and let down. It was as if I'd been punched in the stomach and nobody cared. I retreated into myself. Why hadn't Rachel at least said something to celebrate my accomplishment, the difficulties I overcame in writing a book? Why hadn't Jim reacted to my niece?

And why was my niece's face covered in such sneering anger?

Thinking about it later, I realized that since the publication of my book Fran had kept a distance from me, air kisses replacing real kisses, pseudo warmth where true warmth used to be. Or so I thought.

Maybe I was expecting too much. I reminded myself that this was extended family, if that. I was related by blood only to Rachel, Fran, and Jordan. Perhaps the others didn't consider me to be close enough to require acknowledgement of my accomplishment.

Talk about feeling rejected.

The moment we got into the car, Jim asked if I was okay. "Honey, you'll never reach them," he said. "That's why I didn't say anything. Your book will help people who appreciate your words. Isn't that more important?"

"I wish I had the balls to say how I really felt to Fran and Evan. I wish you had too," I angrily snapped at Jim.

I called Rachel the next day. "Why was your brother-in-law so snarky and defiant when I asked if he'd read my book?" I asked.

Her answer made sense: "Because he loves being a parent. He doesn't want to read about the childfree movement."

I told her that, content aside, it was his tone that surprised me: snide, accusatory, and dismissive. "Honestly, I wanted to see some excitement and pride from you. Aren't you proud of seeing my book in print? Don't you remember all those years I told you how difficult it was writing it? Why didn't you support me?"

Rachel waited a moment before responding. "Well, I've been holding back," she said. "I didn't want to hurt you."

Then she told me why Fran seemed so angry with me, and why she mentioned not wanting to post about the book on Facebook, where Fran had more than five hundred friends.

"Marcia, she doesn't agree with you. She wants kids. Why would you ask her to share it on her Facebook page?"

"Because I thought she would be proud of me," I answered softly. "She doesn't have to agree with my choice, but maybe, just maybe, a few of her friends might be looking for support or questioning motherhood."

"You made her feel uncomfortable," Rachel said. "You made her feel as if she had to do something she didn't want to do and didn't agree with."

Maybe Rachel was right. I didn't want my niece to feel I was forcing her into anything. I only thought she would be excited to share that one of her aunts had published a book.

The day after that phone call with Rachel, I invited my niece for lunch to find out why I detected so much anger and hostility from her. She agreed, but was clearly reluctant.

For privacy, I picked a corner booth at the Corner Café in Tequesta, Florida, a five-minute drive from my sister's home. I waited for Fran with growing apprehension.

She arrived with a bottle of water and said she wasn't hungry when I handed her the menu. That should have been a red flag. Maybe the beach would have been a better meeting place, with more open space and privacy. I suggested it, but she wanted to stay in the restaurant. I ordered a tuna melt on an English muffin. Of the dozens of meals I've eaten there, that's the only specific order I remember.

It's also the only time I didn't eat a single bite.

As soon as I ordered, Fran brought the hammer down: "I'm finally going to tell you how much I don't like you," she sneered.

I was shocked. My thoughts took me back to Fran's childhood, when she would happily run into my arms whenever we saw each other. "Auntie Marcia!" I would hear as she ran toward me and I swept her up into my arms. It was a lovely memory.

However, that wasn't what I faced that day we met for lunch.

Drawing from all the courses about listening and managing anger I had taken in my career as a teacher, I took a deep breath and slowly said, "I'm listening. Why? Why don't you like me?"

That opened the floodgates. Accusation after accusation began pouring out of her. I felt sickened and bewildered. I'd had no clue how deep these hidden feelings ran.

"I've not liked you for a long time, Aunt Marcia!" she

said.

I wondered why Rachel had never told me anything about Fran's feelings. Surely she knew about them. But on second thought I realized that Rachel and I always went out of our way not to rock our boat. She kept me on a pedestal at all costs, and I in turn could never honestly tell her that I felt her kids were overprotected and selfish. We were perfect sisters who never argued.

This is what remains of that painful conversation in my memory, a transcript, like a play I was watching rather than a moment I was living:

Fran: "An aunt is supposed to be cool, like my other aunts. You're not!"

Me: "Why?"

Fran: "It started with that awful self-help book you gave me when I was twelve. Didn't you know it would be hurtful? I mean, who would give a kid a book about facing problems with friends and gaining weight! That wasn't your job! It was my mother's job! Did you ever think you took over her job because you have no kids of your own? You're so controlling."

Me (suppressing the bile working up into my mouth): "I can see how that could upset you. I never meant to hurt you."

Fran: "You always give me that psycho-babble." She mimicked my last statement in a high-pitched voice: "*I can see how that could upset you. I'm sorry. I never mean to hurt you.* Bullshit! None of my other aunts would ever do that! They're just cool aunts. You try and take over my mom's job! Why can't you be like the other four aunts? I love them so much. You don't come near my feelings for them. They just hug me and never try to teach me anything!"

Me: "Do you think I wanted to hurt you?"
Fran: "You're not very smart for a teacher. What aunt does what you've done?"

Me (heart beating so loudly I was sure she could hear it, blood pressure going up, up, up): "Can you give me another example of things I've done that you hated?"

Fran: "Remember when you were coming to visit me at college? The day before you came up, I got last-minute tickets to this awesome rock concert in another city. All my friends were going. I called you and asked if you would mind if I went to that concert instead of taking you on a tour of my campus."

Me: "Of course I remember that. You went to that concert, even though we booked a nearby bed and breakfast. We couldn't wait to see you. When you told us you wouldn't be there, it was too late to cancel and get a refund."

Fran: "What's the big deal? You went anyhow, didn't you? You walked around the campus, didn't you? My other aunts would have understood. Not you! You told me how hurt you were and made me feel guilty!"

Me: "I repeat, we wanted to go to your university, see where you lived, and spend the day with you. We were very disappointed, Fran. That's true. We did feel hurt."

Fran: "I repeat, I'm sure my other aunts would have understood. They wouldn't feel hurt. You don't have kids. They do! You don't get it! They do! And your memoir! I don't agree with your choice. I want you to stop asking me to post about it on my Facebook page!"

I couldn't believe this was happening, all of these bitter feelings I never knew she possessed. I was totally blindsided.

I sat back and said, "Fran, it's true, I never had kids. I only wanted to be a good aunt to you. I can see why I'm not 'cool' to you. I can see why you don't want to post about my book. You've never told me these feelings. Neither did your mom. Can we start over? I'll just be the aunt who hugs you."

Fran sat back into the booth, her face steaming red with anger. She glared at me, and I waited. I had once learned that the one who talks first after an argument usually loses. It was a long wait. Reluctantly, she sighed, rolled her eyes, and said, "I guess so. But I have my doubts about you."

Truth be told, I had my own doubts about her. Her behavior was shockingly immature, offensive, and downright disrespectful. Did I really want to remain in the life of such an angry young woman? Would I like her if she were a neighbor's or a friend's kid? No way. But Fran was family. Family is supposed to mean forever love and forgiveness.

I asked her to pinky-promise she would help me be the aunt she needed and would tell me when she was upset with me so I could try my best to fix it. We locked pinkies and I fought back tears. Tears for myself for being on the receiving end of her intense anger, and tears for her for not appreciating everything I tried to do for her.

I thought about everything Fran said. Was she right that because I never had kids I tried to take over my sister's job, and hadn't realized it? Had I pushed her to share my memoir without even asking about her feelings?

When I question rejection, I tend to do a lot of soul-searching. I've learned to consider the possibility that I'm in some way responsible for that rejection. Because the truth is that sometimes we're at fault, aren't we?

My thoughts traced back to one of my most important role models, my aunt Frieda, and the times we talked, shared, laughed, and enjoyed each other. Frieda would often share her opinions with me. Sometimes I agreed. Many times I didn't, but it didn't matter. We loved each other.

Clearly, Fran didn't love me.

But I felt like I loved her, my only niece. Or had I tricked myself into believing I loved her, just because we're family and society demands there be a bond?

I filtered these rapid thoughts while Fran remained quiet, fooling with her iPhone while I pushed my uneaten tuna melt around my plate. Neither of us spoke.

This quiet was shattered when Fran suddenly slid out of the booth, stood up to glare down at me, and said, "I can't take you anymore. It's useless! I don't need you in my life. You're a controlling narcissist!"

Everyone in the restaurant stopped and stared as out the door she went, slamming it so forcefully I thought the glass window would implode.

Larry, the manager, who I'd come to know well, hustled over to me. Larry had overseen many of my dining experiences at the Corner Café with my sister and friends. He also allowed me to host monthly meetings there for my childfree women's group. That day, he overheard some of my conversation with Fran. "Are you okay?" he whispered.

I wasn't. Tears were about to burst through, and I was doing all I could to keep the dam in place.

Larry quickly boxed my meal and brought the bill.

"Don't let this get to you," he said. "She'll grow up and realize how wrong she is."

I had my doubts. I still do.

Rachel, Fran, and I tried family therapy, but things got even more ugly. At one point, the therapist suggested I ask Fran what she wanted from me. Truly wanting to stop this insanity, I crouched down in front of Fran and asked what I could do to get back into her heart.

Her look was icy. I waited for what seemed like an eternity, until finally she said, "You can go away forever! That's what I want!"

Even the therapist said, "Oh, Fran!" He suggested that Rachel and I continue to work on the rich relationship we'd shared over the years as sisters, and that Fran and I take a break from one another. We all agreed.

My sister and I tried to continue a relationship. We met a few times at the Corner Café, where we talked about things I honestly can't remember. They were the kinds of chit-chatty conversations not worth remembering. I do remember screaming when a baby roach scurried across the floor near us. Larry was beside himself, explaining that he had just had the monthly exterminator, as all restaurants do in Florida. He was shocked that even one roach remained. Rachel and I both laughed, and it felt good. But the sad reality is, we're still estranged. There's been no more shared laughter.

One reason is because of Fran's hatred of me. I feel my sister can't take a chance of losing her. They have a symbiotic relationship. Rachel told me I can't understand because I never had kids. Another reason for the estrangement is that I was at fault for one thing: keeping a journal over many years specifically for my niece and nephew and giving it to them, separately, at their graduations. Fran got one when she graduated college. Jordan got his at his high school graduation party. I wasn't sure I would be around for his college graduation, as I was fighting cancer at the time.

Those journals related every story I knew about them, from their early years to their young adulthood. There were negative things I observed that I never should have included. I should have written those things in my *own* journal, but not shared with them. After rereading Jordan's journal carefully, seeing how negative memories could hurt, I begged for forgiveness. It never was my intention to hurt anyone. Clearly, I did. I finished Jordan's personal journal while doing chemo and radiation. I never had the strength to reread it. I should have. Fran's journal was delivered four years before. She called, in tears, the night of her college graduation. "Aunt Marcia," she gushed, "your journal is the best gift ever!" She didn't make any negative observations. My sister told me later she suggested Fran overlook them at that time.

Rachel told me I was forgiven, but that the incident with the journals was "not forgotten." I understood. I needed to allow time to mend the wounds I created. However, when my birthday went unnoticed until noon on the very day, when we stopped talking in the evenings and stopped wishing each other Happy New Year at the stroke of midnight, when we seemed to talk about nonsense rather than real communication, when she texted me "good luck" while I was in New York for the premiere of the documentary I was in and never asked me how it went, I knew what I had to do.

That rich relationship the therapist spoke of faded into

oblivion. Although I will forever remember the wonderful memories we formed across sixty years of sisterhood and friendship, I now choose to be with people who love and respect me, who forgive me when I'm wrong and love me unconditionally.

In the three years we've been estranged, I've thought about my sister many times. At first, I thought of begging her to come back into my life. Her father, Sid, on his deathbed, whispered, "Marcia, take care of Rachel."

Of course I'll take care of her, I promised. I always had and I would always want to.

That's not how I feel now. I can't take care of someone who doesn't want me in her life. No, I take that back: I *won't* take care of someone who doesn't want me in her life. I'm sure Rachel doesn't want my help anymore, anyway.

After much meditation and many discussions with my husband and close friends, I've come to the conclusion that I may never be able to reach Rachel, Fran, or anyone else who rejects me. They choose to believe I'm a controlling narcissist working to help support "nasty" people who never wanted kids. They believe I breached some unknown aunt rule to only give hugs and to never have conflict. They think I wrote those journals purposefully to hurt them. I couldn't get through to those impenetrable hearts. From their perspective, I will always be at fault. I am the cause, and should forever be punished.

Often I reach for the phone yearning to call my baby sister. I miss our late-night calls. I miss knowing what's happening in her life. I miss my niece and nephew, my brother-in-law and his extended family.

My sister was the only one from her family who

contacted me on my seventy-fifth birthday. She texted, "Happy Birthday," adding several birthday hats and horn emojis. No phone call. No attempt to meet and celebrate, as we'd done in the past. No singing of "Happy Birthday" ending with, "I love you so," as was our birthday ritual in the past. This was my seventy-fifth birthday, a milestone in anyone's life.

I didn't respond to that text. The hurt was too deep.

These three years apart have been painful, but truth be told, there's been more peace in my life. I suspect my sister would say the same thing. My nephew, Jordan, hasn't seen me since he graduated high school. Knowing that he was in his final year of college, I sent him a text wishing him the best of luck in his last year. No response. I imagine he doesn't want to rock the boat with his sister. They had a contentious relationship until a few years ago. I'm sure he doesn't want to face her wrath. By the way, he never read that infamous journal.

At night, before I go to sleep, I send my sister and her family loving thoughts to heal their hearts. I hope they're well and happy. It eases my pain, and it helps me feel like I'm still that big sister looking out for my baby sister. I'm sure Rachel and her family would call that a sign of my narcissism or having to be in control. On some level, they're right: not about me being a narcissist, but about me taking control by sending them good wishes. It brings me peace.

I abandoned the myth that my family will love me unconditionally. My sister said, "I placed you on a pedestal! It's now broken." I don't want to be on any pedestal. Statues are placed on pedestals, where they're subject to being pooped on by pigeons. Statues are unfeeling, rigid, never changing, and incapable of verbal communication. I want to be seen as a human who sometimes makes mistakes.

When I realized I wasn't being forgiven for the things I wrote in those journals and wasn't being invited to family events, I felt profoundly disappointed and hurt. What happened to those times I was there for my sister and her family? Those times I obviously cared? Those times I didn't make a stupid mistake? I found myself repeating these thoughts over and over. The result was an awful feeling in the depth of my being.

When I changed the negative thoughts reverberating in my brain to help me accept where Rachel was and let her go, I felt better.

Do I still care about my sister? Sure. We both have season tickets to the Kravis Theater in West Palm Beach, Florida. She told me it would be best if I remain in the mezzanine and don't come to the orchestra area, where she has a cup of coffee during intermission. Her reasoning was that it might be too "awkward" for everyone should we bump into each other. Sigh.

We're born into families. Sometimes it's not a good fit. When we choose what we want and who we want to share our lives with, we regain control. Although rejection by our family may still hurt because of the old "blood is thicker than water" myth, love, positive thinking, and genuine support from caring people can often ease the pain.

****

It's not just family members who may reject us for

choosing a childfree lifestyle. Sometimes, people we thought were lifelong friends may be the source of terrible, bewildering rejection if they don't support our choice to remain childfree. Many times, they genuinely love being a parent and want us to feel the same thing. Although well-meaning, their enthusiasm can fall on deaf ears when not everyone sees pregnancy, birth, and the parenting lifestyle in the same way. Repetitive arguments may result in rejection and the end of those long-term friendships.

If you choose to retaliate with harsh words out of frustration, it may lead to a push-pull dance of, "I'm right, you're wrong."

Friend: "Why don't you want kids?"

You: "Don't like the whole lifestyle."

Friend: "What if you regret it when it's too late?"

You: "I'd rather regret it than have kids and regret them!"

Friend: "That's ridiculous! Parents love their kids!"

You: "I really hope that's true for you!"

On and on continues the dysfunctional cha cha cha of trying to be right. Nobody wins!

If your own friends don't accept you just the way you are, you have the power to change your attitude toward them to release yourself from their ill-conceived perceptions. Remember, it's perceptions and expectations that make people respond. It's not about you. You're not selfish. You're not immature. You won't change your mind or regret your choice. Maybe they will, though one would never wish that on a parent.

I suggest that instead of becoming a victim of bullying or harassing friendships, you re-evaluate whether the friends you once loved are actually the friends you have now. That may mean taking a break from them to see how they miss you, or if you miss them. If that doesn't happen, maybe they weren't true friends?

This is why I've repeated the importance of finding like-minded people in the childfree community. It eases or can sooth the intense emotional pain of feeling rejected by others. Meetup.com may offer support groups in your area. Internationally, finding such a community may be more challenging. If there aren't any, see if you can create your own. Or join one of the many support groups on Facebook, Instagram, or Twitter. Simply place the word "childfree" in the search bar. You'll be amazed how many there are.

Here's what I learned over seventy-six years: you can't change people's minds, misperceptions, or expectations. It's up to those who fiercely hold on to those misperceptions and expectations to decide if they want to let go and see things in a different light. The important thing is how those expectations affect us.

Is it painful to be rejected for a personal thought, belief, or lifestyle? You bet it is. Can it lead us to feel sadness, hurt, or bewilderment? Sadly, yes. Might we even start rethinking, asking ourselves if we need to change to fit the accepted, revered way of living? It sure would be easier, wouldn't it? However we would lose who we really are. In my opinion, that would be the biggest loss. You can't lead a life based on what other people want you to do. People always seem to want us to live according to their idea of right and wrong. Isn't our own right or wrong important?

I've embraced Maya Angelou's suggestion that "If you don't like something, change it. If you can't change it, change your attitude."

It's cathartic to change your thoughts about rejection. I recognized the need to feel rejection, experience it, then let it go. If you experience the experience, the experience goes away. It doesn't mean it's totally gone. It means that after you've cried, or wished for better choices from people, the hurtful rejection diminishes until it doesn't feel acute anymore.

I cried when I felt that gut-wrenching rejection by my family. Ranted! Beat a pillow! The best place I ranted was in my car with the windows closed tight. Then I wrote down the hurt I felt. I took those feelings, written on paper, to the beach, lit a match, and watched them disintegrate into the atmosphere. It's freeing to let go of rejection and people in your life who feel toxic or draining.

I think of friends who still reject me. It's offered me a profound lesson, maybe even a gift. It teaches me the value of knowing who my friends really are. When I get tons of texts, phone calls, cards, invitations to lunch or dinner, and gifts on my birthday, it's heartwarming. On days when I have those dreaded PET scans to make sure the cancer is gone and people check in to see how I'm doing, it shows me blood is *not* always thicker than water, and true friendships stay true!

****

Recently, I was honored to be included in Maxine Trump's (no relation to Donald) documentary *To Kid or Not To Kid*. In this provocative and inspirational film, Maxine shares her journey from childless to childfree by choice. The film also deals with the loss of her best friend over something Maxine said. She told her friend she thought people having large families were selfish, given the ravages of overpopulation. Her friend was insulted. She planned on having more children! The friend totally rejected her. Although Maxine tried again and again to reach her, they never reunited.

Maxine found me through the Internet. We talked a lot about the proposed film. When she heard I had a best friend of forty-five years who is a mother of two sons and accepted my choice to remain childfree, she wanted to film us.

On the day Jane and I were filmed, Maxine had us facing each other and looking into each other's eyes. Maxine whispered, "Don't speak. Just keep looking at each other." Suddenly we both started tearing up! They weren't sad tears. They were joyous tears expressing how much our friendship meant to us.

That scene was cut. However, what was included was an interview with me about the *60 Minutes* fiasco. She also filmed Jane and me suggesting that perhaps the friend who rejected her wasn't a true friend. Jane ended the scene by saying, "Find a friend who loves you unconditionally."

There are times you need to protect your boundaries from your family or your friends. If you're facing more and more accusations with more and more vitriol, it may be time to wish people well and leave. If at every family function or meeting with friends you're labeled selfish, irresponsible, or an embarrassment because of your personal choice, it's probably time to stop going to those functions. If you keep hearing how your own sister's or brother's kids mean the world to your parents, and how you're selfishly letting them down by not giving them more grandchildren, it may be time to stop visiting. If you're told you're not in the will because you don't have kids, that your brother or sister who has kids needs the money more than you, it may be time to move on. If you're infertile, and you've announced to your family that you're not childless but rather childfree by choice, and still they say, yet again, "But you can adopt," or "But you can try another IVF treatment," it may be time to stop engaging them in conversation.

There's a peace that comes with taking a stand and sticking to it. Even when that stand is estrangement from those you care about, you're showing love to yourself. That's not narcissistic. That's simply taking care of your own inner child. There's a welcome sense of completion that comes when you decide to no longer be anyone's victim.

If you can't respect your choices and value yourself, who will?

This isn't as easy as I make it sound. Even I, after all these years as an outspoken advocate for the childfree lifestyle, sometimes succumb to my own negative thoughts when it comes to rejection by family and friends. I've heard it said that we teach what we're most in need of learning. I may have to read this book a few times myself! Hopefully, then, rejection loses.

Chapter 2
Pronatalism

"If you are writing about baloney, don't try and make it Cornish hen, because that's the worst kind of baloney there is. Just make it darn good baloney."
— Leo Burnett

In 1973 the word "pronatalism" entered my personal lexicon. I learned the meaning of this word after reading Ellen Peck's scandalous (for the time) 1971 book, *The Baby Trap*. It was the first time I'd read anything that catapulted me into realizing my life didn't have to include anything called motherhood. There was no other book of any kind that referred to babies as traps.

When I came to the last page, the relief was instantaneous. It felt like the afterglow to good sex with a much-needed release! I wasn't an aberration of a psychologically troubled woman. I no longer thought of myself as different from the norm. I was, according to Ellen, a whole and perfectly sane woman. In fact, I was smart, maybe smarter than those who chose to have a baby just because it's the norm. I was finally free from thoughts that I had to be a mother—thoughts that made me shiver with distaste. Child-rearing was a personal choice, not a requirement. Child-freedom was a viable, personally rewarding alternative to raising humans! I was thirty-two. I had probably wrestled with whether or not I was normal for sixteen years.

I never knew what pronatalism was before reading Ellen's book. I'd never heard the word. It was kind of fun to say it: *pro-nate-a-lism*. I emphasized the consonant sounds. It made me feel smarter, because hardly anyone had ever heard of it. I may have used it too many times, just to hear it and see the reactions of people who said, "Say what?"

I was glib in answering. "You never heard of pronatalism? It means exalting the status of birth or parenting while diminishing those who don't hold that title." I would smile after saying that. Okay, I admit it. I was overdoing it a bit. It wasn't a mean streak. It was just the beginning of my passion to make the childfree lifestyle as accepted as parenting. I wanted to point out the many ways we're brainwashed and trapped into thinking parenting must be a part of our life experience. It started me on the path to becoming a pioneer in the childfree movement.

I was breathless to share examples from Ellen's book with anyone who was remotely interested. Her revelations showed how businesses and advertisers helped create the cultural primacy of birth and babies. They could sell more products that way! It wasn't just toy manufacturers, either. One example Ellen provided was the Equitable Life Insurance Society, which in 1971 offered a program to help families meet "projected future needs." Ellen wrote:

"And, just to make sure there's no doubt about what that means and as a come-on to help make those projected future needs occur in the near future, an Equitable ad shows a gal standing regally, beside a harp (!), one hand protectively over her expanding stomach" (pg. 23, *The Baby Trap*).

I quickly showed people how that insurance company made more money off higher premiums, with more and more babies added to a family policy. It also not so subtly promoted pregnancy by placing a woman next to a harp as an angel! Any woman looking at that ad was encouraged to see herself standing by that ridiculous harp, serenely pregnant. They're special. They're important. They're women treasured by everyone.

I went on a hunt for ads selling more than a product. I found a Campbell's Soup ad in a magazine. One line said, "It's not soup 'til mother makes it!" Really? I made that soup many times on cold winter nights in New York. If it wasn't soup 'til mother makes it, then what the hell did I heat up for my husband and me? That's what I wrote to that soup company. They sent me back a letter apologizing for any offense and assuring me I was serving terrific soup even though I wasn't a mom. They also sent me a carton of Campbell's tomato soup!

Although I appreciated the soup, I felt placated, as if the adverting gurus at Campbell's were saying, "There, there, Marcia. Be a good woman and forget this." The apology was for my taking offense, not for their responsibility in making that pronatalistic ad. I was sure I would see more ads using mothers cooking to promote products. And I did, and still do.

In the first few chapters of Ellen's book, the reality of pronatalism rears its ugly head and, at the same time, made me do my happy dance. Reading those chapters opened my eyes wider and wider. Her shocking revelations about how manufacturers, the media, music, art, and cultural expectations brainwash us into thinking anything pro-birth is to be revered truly stunned me. It was shocking. She helped me understand why I thought I needed therapy. I was supposed to want to be a mother! Everything showed that. Everyone supported that.

Yet, when I tried to explain the damages of pronatalism to other people, nothing seemed to register. Pronatalism rocked on in their minds and hearts. Of course ads reflect the normalcy of having children. Most people have kids! Kids mean more money to businesses. "What's the big deal?" people asked. Of course music and the arts depict the Madonna-and-baby theme. It's lovely! It makes mothers feel honored, as many should be. It reflects the joys of motherhood. Most agreed that raising children is the epitome of life's experiences. To miss out on it would make life meaningless.

The No. 1 song in America in 1974 was Paul Anka's "You're Having My Baby." People swooned over the lyrics:

"You're having my baby/

What a lovely way of saying/

How much you love me."

I cringed when I heard that song played over and over on every radio channel. Couldn't I show love to my husband without a baby? Then I had an epiphany. This was that dangerous song Ellen spoke of. It made having a baby the proof of loving someone. Paul Anka never considered the harm this song might do. How many women who couldn't have children felt rejected as barren? How many women wanted that baby so they could fit the image the song portrayed to family, friends, and co-workers. The lyrics even suggest the woman could have aborted that baby, but chose life instead. She was a sainted martyr.

Ellen Peck's next book, co-authored with Judith Senderowitz, was *Pronatalism: The Myth of Mom & Apple Pie*. It was a more in-depth exploration of pronatalism. This book was published in 1974, during my awakening. I read both *The Baby Trap* and this second book in that infamous year of 1974. I devoured this second book during the time I helped Ellen on that first NON (National Organization for Non-Parents) convention in New York City. After reading *The Baby Trap*, I saw an ad at the end of that book announcing a monthly NON meeting in New York City, with a phone number. I went to the next meeting with my husband and became very, very active. Even though it was a long trip from Long Island into Manhattan, I loved being with this new and accepting tribe. That's where I met Ellen Peck. That's how I decided to volunteer to help her with the first NON convention.

My life was filled with learning everything I could about what I came to recognize as a movement to acknowledge the non-parenting lifestyle as a viable alternative to parenting. I was thirty-two.

This second pronatalism book added details the first book didn't cover. Twenty-four chapters exposed how women's magazines and romance novels glorified mothering, how TV soaps presented marriages with babies as more successful, how home economics textbooks in schools ignored the raw realities of raising children, how attitudes toward childlessness promoted the idea that a marriage without children is doomed to fail, and so much more information undermining the myth that having and raising babies is the most amazing, wonderful lifestyle.

This second book gave me more examples of the brainwashing I was raised on as a young woman in the late '40s and early '50s, when I had my dolls, played "house," and fought over the title of "Mom" when playing with my friends. During my middle-school years, I took a class on home economics. We were taught how to sew, cook, and take care of our future families. (The boys were segregated to "shop" class, where they made wooden shelves.) I remember seeing in the required textbook a photo of a man sitting on a lounge chair. The photo's caption said, "Make sure your children are washed and fed before your husband comes home. Greet him with his slippers and a hot meal." It was a sad reflection of terrible pronatalism and misogyny, based on the assumption that I would surely raise children and be a slave to my life partner, too.

Thanks to the women's movement and feminism, the social expectation that a woman should be a slave to a man is almost gone. The exception would be in some strict religious practices. Now, with the ascent of the "Me Too" generation, women are taking more of a stand about how they're treated. Sitting back and not speaking truths about sexual exploitation is no longer acceptable. Pronatalism, however, rocks on!

In my memoir, published in 2013, I contributed to the conversation about pronatalism. The most revealing awakening arrived with my interview on *60 Minutes*, a widely respected and viewed American TV show. The aftermath of that broadcast, including the loss of my teaching career and picketers and death threats when I spoke, spurred me on to become a childfree activist. I never thought such fear and hatred could be aimed at anyone for simply making a personal lifestyle choice! I still get emails from people saying they can't believe what I went through. I hope Chapter 3, "60 Minutes," helped people to be more open, honest, and proud in stating their personal lifestyle choices. I don't believe anyone would lose a job these days for choosing a childfree lifestyle, because it would clearly be seen as discrimination. In 1974, I didn't have the nerve to fight the school district that "excessed" me. They told me they had too many teachers. Since I was the last hired, I had to go.

Another chapter I enjoyed writing in my memoir chronicled my experience with a man I met after my divorce from my first husband. Peter was strictly against having "chabbies," as he called children. (I have no idea where he got that word!) In my naiveté as a woman, in the late 1960s, still not at peace with choosing a childfree lifestyle, I recoiled! Pronatalism (although I didn't know the word then) taught me this was a selfish, perhaps immature man. Although I had absolutely no thoughts of remarriage after an upsetting divorce, my mom almost had me sending him away! She said, "He's not marriage material. Don't waste your time." My mom couldn't see dating for any other reason than to find another husband and have a family.

I went against Mom's warning. We were a couple for almost two years. There was something about Peter that felt good during that time. He didn't want marriage. He didn't want a family. He was fun, sexy, and adorable. He was one of the best parts of my life. Our breakup was mutual. He needed more "lobster and fried clams," not a diet of filet mignon every night. I giggled at that sentence. Hey! I could have been a bowl of chili! Right? It really was Pete's desire to experience other women that made me know our time together as a couple was ending.

Two years later, when he heard I had married a man who supported me in not wanting to have children, he couldn't stop laughing. "You? You who said, 'What? How

45

could anyone not want a child?' You're now a staunch advocate of that lifestyle? I think I'm going to pee in my pants from laughing!"

Peter and I remained friends throughout his life. We never missed a single birthday, though separated by many, many miles. I lost him to an illness, and miss his laughter and friendship. I'm thankful that the pronatalism that poisoned my mom's attitude toward Peter, and almost poisoned my own mind, never stopped me from experiencing Peter. He came into my life at the right time. We remained dear friends in our forever hearts.

Peter also provided a lesson in being true to your own heart. I needed and wanted Peter. Had I listened to Mom's pronatalistic version of why Peter wasn't right for me, I might never have known his joy in my life. When others tell you you're making a mistake by staying with someone who doesn't want kids, it can be a deal-breaker! If your partner suddenly decides they want kids and you still do not, walk away. Remember the good and let them go.

In my memoir, I talked about menopause. Pronatalism taught me I would ache for the baby I didn't have once it was too late and I couldn't become pregnant. I did find sadness when I realized there were no eggs left! But my sadness wasn't for any baby I never made or raised. It was because I no longer had any *choice* in the matter. Although I never wanted to change my mind, I always felt I had the option. Now, "the end" loomed before me: the end of my period, the end of cramps and Midol, the end of seeing the blood coming from me, knowing I now faced the realities of being older. Now, death seemed to raise its ugly head.

During this time, I became clear how pronatalism affected my vision of "the change." Instead of seeing it as a celebration of one of life's passages, I feared wrinkled skin, hair on my face, and drooping breasts. The lesson was in seeing that women who birthed children endured wrinkled skin, hair on their face, and drooping breasts as well. Not having children or grandchildren, I had more time to lather my skin with lotions and have my face cared for by an esthetician. And I actually still had firm breasts because I never breastfed! My life didn't stop at menopause. The biological clock stopped, and it felt good.

In 2012, Laura Carroll, author of *Families of Two*, wrote *The Baby Matrix*, subtitled *Why Freeing Our Minds From Outmoded Thinking About Parenthood and Reproduction Will Create a Better World*. I devoured this book. Laura, who became a sister-friend of mine, goes into the details of how pronatalism continues, and why it's still so dangerous. She speaks of many assumptions we see globally about how everyone should experience having and raising a child. Even though we all know many people aren't parent material, the assumptions reign supreme. Here's her list of those assumptions:

1. It's a destiny.
2. It's normal.
3. Children always follow marriage.
4. It's everyone's right and obligation to reproduce.
5. Fulfillment automatically comes with having children.
6. Old age is a lonely experience without children.

Pronatalism presumes that everyone will or should have children in their lives. I decided to go on a hunt to see how pronatalism is still a major force today. It didn't take long to find many examples!

Remember Paul Anka's "You're Having My Baby"?

Here's my 2019 pronatalistic award song: "I Believe Most People Are Good," by Luke Bryan. Here's the refrain:

I believe most people are good
And most mamas oughta qualify for sainthood
I believe most Friday nights look better under neon or
stadium lights
I believe you love who you love
Ain't nothing you should ever be ashamed of
I believe this world ain't half as bad as it looks
I believe most people are good.

Now, don't get mad with me. Although the rest of this song is a bit sappy, it's not that bad. With one exception:
"I believe most people are good and most mamas ought to qualify for sainthood."

That one pronatalistic line is dangerous! Okay, he does use the word "most." Years ago, it might have read "all." It's a step in the right direction, but I still consider it dangerously pronatalistic, and an example of how pronatalism rocks on. It places the title of mother under sainthood! It dismisses those of us who don't want, can't have, or shouldn't have children. Yet, many of those very women who are not mothers are "saints" in their own lives.

Does praising mothers diminish non-mothers? I think it does. Think about it. Anyone who shows a pregnant belly automatically gets accolades. Can she afford it? Doesn't matter. Is she parent material? Doesn't matter. Is this the fourth child? Doesn't matter. Shrieks of joy or applause come when announcements are made at work or at family gatherings. Anyone who has a baby in their arms is deemed special, whether or not that's their truth. That's how they're perceived.

Non-mothers aren't acknowledged. They can be leaders in animal protection. Doesn't matter. Not the same as raising a child. They can be wonderfully committed teachers. Doesn't matter. They aren't mothers. They can be politically active in fighting climate change or other causes. Doesn't matter. They can simply be caring humans making their lives or the lives they touch happier. Doesn't matter. They can be pursuing higher education or a skill needed to help others. Doesn't matter. Doesn't come near being a mother.

And now, being a father!

A recent billboard in my neighborhood for a political candidate showed the man and his child. Under his picture it read, "Dads can be a good example of a great man!" Okay. It used the word "can." But what words stay in your mind?" "Dads," "great," and "man." Pronatalism rocks on for men, too!

I turned on the TV searching for rampantly pronatalistic ads. In no time I saw the following ad for a car, touching on Laura Carroll's "It's a destiny" and "Children always follow marriage" and "Fulfillment automatically comes with having children" pronatal assumptions.

Scene: A lovely pregnant woman tenderly caresses her belly while speaking to her unborn child. She speaks of the beauty of oceans. Then you see her walking through a forest talking to her unborn child about the joy of forests.

Next scene: A ten-year-old girl happily gets out of the family's ten-year-old Subaru and runs to the sea. Mom and Dad smile with joy as they watch her seemingly happy experience at the beach, and hug each other as their child runs to the water.

What's so wrong about that? They're teaching about nature, you may think. Agreed. It's good to show the joys of our planet, but there's a lot more being taught. Here are some subtle messages that creep into many unconscious minds unaware of pronatalism.

1. All pregnant women adore their pregnancies and take time to lovingly speak to their unborn child. What about the many women who have terrible or unwanted pregnancies, who vomit, who have hemorrhoids falling out of their anus, who can't sleep and suffer from many other bodily challenges associated with pregnancy?

2. All women have men who are there for them and their child. How many women are single moms? Or have partners who leave the raising of their children to the women?

3. All children grow up loving what their parents love. Seriously?

4. All parents have cars and the time to take their children to the beach and share in that experience. How many use public transportation because they are poor and can't afford a car because raising a child is a financial burden?

As bad as this example is, there was one good thing: the ad showed only one child. Most pronatalistic ads from the past had at least two kids, one boy and one girl. The girl in that recent TV car ad wasn't a baby, either. She was a pre-teen. You get the feeling there are no more kids to come. Maybe the reality of this planet's population explosion hit the advertiser for this car? This would be a good thing.

There's another TV car ad I kind of giggled at. It's pronatalistic, but it does show some of the realities of having children. You see a woman in the front seat, looking at the rearview mirror and saying in an exasperated voice: "Okay! Stop it now! Don't fight with your sister! I'm going to turn this car around if you don't stop!"

The camera pans to two adults in the backseat of that car staring without expression. They seem speechless. They're bewildered salespeople helping the woman take this car for an apparent test drive. She says, "It feels good. I'll take it!" It's a pronatalistic ad, as she's depicted talking to her two children, who of course will be in that car when she gets home. But at least some of the frustrating realities that most parents face are included. This is a step in the right direction.

More present day-ads support Laura Carroll's prenatal assumption that "It's normal."

There are tons of current magazine ads showing a mom and her child or children using products. And not necessarily products relating to children, either. Mr. Clean ran a magazine ad showing a mom and her daughter smiling as the mom uses the Mr. Clean magic sponge. Of course it's "normal" to have only a mother figure cleaning, and not a father figure, although I have lately seen more men using cleaning products with children. The smiling little girl is right there with her mom, lovingly watching her clean. Reality? Most kids have no interest in helping their parents clean unless they're getting paid. Most moms have very little time to enjoy cleaning. Their lives are overfilled with the endless responsibilities of raising their families, taking care of their home, and working.

Other ads support Carroll's pronatal assumption that "Old age is a lonely experience without children." A popular ad right now on TV shows a scenario in which a family is preparing for the addition in their home of another family member. The parents talk to their financial adviser, who says, "I know you've been waiting a long time to make this happen." The viewer thinks they're preparing for another child. Nope. The next scene shows them welcoming their mother or mother-in-law. "Welcome home, Mom!" is heard as they tenderly open the door and let her in.

How is this pronatalism? It incorrectly makes people think that as we age, our children will be there to support us. The facts simply don't bear this out. This type of ad can frighten people into falsely believing that if they have no children, they'll have no one to help them in their old age. The truth is that this is happening to many parents. Visit any nursing home or assisted-living facility and you'll see many aging people sitting alone.

I grew up without the Internet. Today, the world is flush with prenatal messaging via the Internet. This morning, one of my followers sent me perhaps the most disturbing video ever shared on a mommy Facebook site. It's a video of a real little girl, maybe two years old, cradling her baby sister and trying to breastfeed her. The baby is wailing. In the background you hear a voice—I'm assuming it's the mother—saying, "Good job! She's getting it!"

I actually felt sick to my stomach. To me, it's offensive and deeply disturbing. Here's a young child already being programmed to believe it will be her job to feed a child. What's next? Model sexual intercourse to show how it's done? That baby was hungry. Making the two-year-old attempt to feed her baby sister borders on perverse and, perhaps, abuse of the screaming baby in need of feeding. Several of my Facebook followers reported this video to Facebook. The answer came back that it conforms to Facebook's guidelines. There was no place to explain to any Facebook representative why this video was so dangerous.

Yesterday, standing in line at the supermarket, I overheard the cashier in adamantly pronatalistic conversation with her food bagger.

"Of course you'll have kids!" the cashier said as her bagger placed bananas into the plastic shopping bag.

"Nope. Don't think so," the bagger said as he reached for a box of cereal to add to the bag.

"You're young!" the casher said, turning to look at the bagger with an expression of growing annoyance. She continued: "You'll change your mind when you meet the right woman. You'll see!"

The bagger shook his head slowly left and right, his face turning red. I had the feeling he wanted to jump into the packages and disappear. He didn't respond.

The cashier went in for the kill: "You should have at least two!"

That's when I lost it. I shouted, "Listen. This is his choice, not a destiny for him. We have enough children on this planet. If he doesn't want kids, please leave him alone. I wrote a book on this topic."

The cashier stopped. Her head was swiveling left and right from the man to me. She then fixated on me, saying, "I bless those who say they don't want children. Why do we insist everyone have them?"

In my head, I thought, *Say what? You've been insisting he should have kids, and now you're blessing me for not?* Taking the high road, I simply said, "Can I hug you?"

"Of course," she said, and came around to give me a hug.

The young man who bagged my groceries walked me out to the car, pushing my food carriage. (It's a complimentary service from this food chain in Florida.)

"Congratulations," I said, walking beside the shopping cart to my car. "You just witnessed your first bout of pronatalism."

The young man said, "What's that?"

Keeping up with his fast stride toward my car, I offered: "Exalting the status of parenting. Belittling the ones who say they never want the experience."

He stopped the cart and slowly said, "Hell no! I'm going to be a pilot and travel the world. Never wanted kids. Won't change my mind!"

Pronatalism can occur anywhere, not just in ads. It creates havoc in religions that deem children to be a blessing from God! How do those couples who can't procreate due to infertility feel? They're not blessed? How do people who should never have kids due to genetic challenges feel when they marry and hear, "Bless this couple with children"?

Yesterday, I saw a shared post on one of my childfree sites. It was a plea to advertisers to stop normalizing child-rearing as fulfillment while devaluing those who don't procreate, either by choice or due to infertility. The ad showed a woman elated about a positive pregnancy test. (The pregnancy test was the product.) The poster suggested a different kind of ad: "Normalize women not being baby incubators by showing them in a pregnancy test commercial *celebrating* negative results!"

I wish I could tell you, dear reader, that pronatalism has lost its hold on us. Sadly, we can't pop the champagne bottles yet. It's been more than forty years since I first flaunted that five-syllable word, feeling a bit cocky knowing most people had never heard of it. I'm sure pronatalism was around long before I knew what the word meant. Actually, even now, that important word is still not heard as much as it should be. I still get a red line under it every time I type "pronatalism" on my computer, suggesting the spelling is wrong, because it's not a known word. Sometimes it's replaced with the word "prenatal." I giggle every time I see that.

Although the number of people choosing not to have children is on the rise, pronatalism rocks on, even as our world population is exploding. It's a never-ending phenomenon glorifying birth and exalting the status of parenting. Having children is still an expected outcome of marriage and partnering. Even in the LGBTQ community, children are an expected outcome. From what gay people tell me, partners who adopt children or have a child through surrogacy are given more respect and acceptance than those who do not have children.

We now see more ads with biracial children, single parents, and adopted children. That shows a shift in the idea of what makes a family. I've also seen ads for dog food using the words "pet parents." However, ads, the media, music, art, and movies have not stopped the societal brainwashing that depicts having children as life's purpose.

Right now, our planet has more than seven billion

humans. Our planet can effectively sustain two billion. Yet, nothing seems to stop the progression toward having children as the ultimate outcome in everyone's life. It's people's right. It's the joy of life. It's the expectation of friends, family, neighbors, and co-workers.

So what can you do to illuminate and teach the dangers of pronatalism?

1. Speak up! If you see anything pronatalistic, take a stand and be that stand, like I did on that grocery store checkout line. Write to pronatalistic advertisers. Tell them how their ads are dangerously promoting a destiny that's not necessarily good for everyone, or for our over-populated planet.

2. Speak up in your family. Stay loud and proud of your awesome choice to remain childfree.

3. Speak up at work. Don't allow pronatalistic policies to overwork you without pay when you have to take over the job of a parent. (Unless you get equal treatment when you have to care for an ailing family member or pet!)

4. Speak up in your schools. Ask your school board to make sure your school teaches realistic texts addressing the planet's population explosion and whether parenting is the best choice for everyone.

5. Speak up! Use the word "pronatal" as often as you can to raise the consciousness of those who have no clue about the dangers of pronatalism.

6. If you have friends who are parents and they confide how exhausted or disillusioned they are, speak up! Tell them it's because pronatalism kept them from the truth. They have a right to be upset. If they need professional help, suggest parenting courses or a good therapist to cope with the realities of raising children.

We need to end pronatalism if we truly care about this planet and the children of the future. Too many children are being born into awful experiences because their parents were manipulated into thinking parenting is a biological or societal destiny. Too many parents are now admitting that maybe, just maybe, they were never parent material, but felt pressured to have children.

It's time for us to become proud and loving warriors against the myths promoted by pronatalism. Pronatalism causes most of the heartbreaking rejection experienced by so many, as you will read in the following chapters. The more we speak up, the more we can help to overcome pronatalism. Our voices and our pride in the childfree lifestyle are our power. Together, as a proactive and passionate force, we can fight to end pronatalism. It can't march on when it's been seen as what it is: a danger to the right to make choices that are best for ourselves.

Chapter 3
Promises Not Kept

"Broken vows are like broken mirrors. They leave those who held to them bleeding and staring at fractured images of themselves."
—Richard Paul Evans

When I saw her on Skype, her brown eyes were welling up with tears. They were about to cascade down her cheeks into a puddle. I saw a crumpled tissue in her hand, anticipating the bursting dam of emotions. Her dark hair was pulled back in a tight ponytail. A few loose tendrils cascaded down her face. The telltale signs of crying had not fully begun. No mascara stained her face. It would be there soon. I guessed her to be in her late twenties.

I gently welcomed Anna and acknowledged the pain and sadness I knew she was feeling. This Internet meeting was the result of a private message she'd sent via one of my Facebook support sites for the childfree:

"Marcia, I need your help. I've been in a committed relationship. We were planning on getting married. He knew I never wanted kids and agreed. Now, three years later, he says he changed his mind. He's trying to get me to feel guilty because I don't want to have his child. I can't believe this is happening. He says it's normal to want a kid when you're in love. I feel rejected. It's making me think maybe I should change my mind and give him that child! I'm afraid I'll never find another person I love who doesn't want kids."

For many childfree-by-choice people, it's difficult to

find a life partner who isn't filled with the romantic myth of babies equating to proof of profound love. I thought back many times to the irony of a song my second husband wrote for me. At the time, I thought it was touching. Mathew picked up his guitar, sat down before me, looked into my eyes, and sang a syrupy sort of country-western song. He sang of his never-ending love. (It's funny to me now, knowing our marriage ended with his having an affair.) Then came a line I still giggle at: he pictured me on a back porch with a baby in my arms. My eyes filled with tears. After my mentally abusive first marriage, which ended in a welcomed divorce, here was a dream come true. Here was a man who loved and treasured me. It fit the ideal and expectation of marriage. It warmed my heart thinking of giving him a child... with a bit of apprehension that I cast aside. Did I really want his child? We were poor and couldn't afford to have children. I had an excuse, at least for a while. Neither of us had seen the light yet back in 1972, before reading *The Baby Trap* in 1974. Neither of us admitted we truly didn't think we wanted kids. However, his song was written to move me, which it did, and perhaps to prove something to himself. Maybe it was a test to see my reaction? Or just a line in a song to affect me the way he was taught it would. In those days, you never discussed having or not having a child. It was just expected. Luckily, our story ended happily, at least for a while, after reading Ellen's book. We gratefully learned that neither of us wanted to parent. However, we later divorced after eight years of marriage.

Too many other couples face the reality of one partner wanting a child when the other doesn't.

Anna, however, clearly thought she and her boyfriend

were in total agreement. She revealed that they often laughed when their friends complained about the challenges of raising kids: lack of money, lack of sleep, and lack of sex, not necessarily in that order. She dryly quipped, "That wasn't going to happen to us."

I told Anna she wasn't the first person with this challenge and wouldn't be the last. Our intense conversation centered on a lot of what follows in this chapter. I asked her if I could post her issue on my childfree Facebook site. She agreed. It generated a tsunami of comments. I wrote this post:

"How many of you ever had a love relationship, based on mutual agreements, to live a childfree lifestyle, only to face your beloved changing their mind? How did that feel? What did you do?"

Many of the comments were similar to Troy's: "We ended it. I'm firm in my conviction. Always have. Always will be."

People who can simply walk away from a relationship when the goals have changed are very determined and self-assured. They usually won't cave in to another person's wants or needs. I'm not suggesting there aren't feelings of disappointment. Of course, there may be. However, they're determined not to live a lifestyle caring for children. They recognize that people can change their minds, and steadfastly move on feeling secure they can find another life partner. Or they feel certain their lives will be fine without any life partner. In either case, they're extremely committed to the childfree lifestyle. For them, it's a short stay in sadness. Letting go is their relief.

Here's another response from a self-assured man:

Adam: "No! She didn't shame me. It's not like I wasn't

61

vocal about my desire *not* to have and raise children. Some things I'm willing to make concessions with, but having children isn't one of them. I kind of gave up on dating for a while because I didn't trust people under 30. They often talked a similar talk, but after about 8 months, the conversation changes to, 'You really don't want kids?'

"I'm not willing to sacrifice my own happiness for someone else's future!

"So, I remained single for eight years. I'm now with someone who I know won't change her position on children. She had her tubes tied. Mature love is everything."

Others know they never want to have children, but say nothing until they're sure it's a real possibility in a forever partnership. Childfree-by-choice people may be fearful of sharing that lifestyle choice out of concern they'll not be accepted as partner material. Sometimes they hold off, hoping to talk and overcome all the exaggerated hype and myths about raising children. They fear the rejection. Of course, if rejection is coming, it's better to know that up front than to wait for months or years to find out.

Sometimes, people are very up-front and honest. They'll state their goals in a relationship and clearly share their desire to remain childfree by choice. Many times, the other person will think, *Oh! Pfffff! I can change that!* Some who are on the fence will cave in and reconsider parenting, as Anna did. She was in love. She was almost persuaded by the myth that a child is the ultimate gift of love. She even said, "Marcia, maybe it's worth having a baby to keep him. Maybe I'll really enjoy it after all! Everyone says once you hold that baby, you're in love with it." I reminded her that many parents now say that's a myth. Many parents don't have that feeling. Many suffer overwhelming stress when reality hits.

In our Skype communication, Anna and I went over the demands she would face as a parent. She admitted the thought of pregnancy turned her off cold. "You know that's part of having a child unless you adopt?" I asked.

"Nope! He never wants another person's kid." Anna flicked a tendril of hair from her sweet face. When I asked if she thought he would be her equal in parenting their child, she was defiant. "Hell no! He's told me raising the baby is a *woman's* job. He would be the one making the money. I would be the one taking care of the child and doing the chores in the home."

I asked Anna what she did for work. She excitedly told me she had a job with an advertising company and was starting to work her way up to a more lucrative position. She loved what she did and couldn't wait to get to her job each day.

"Do you hear what you're telling me?" I softly asked. There was a long pause. She just stared into the Skype camera, nervously biting her lower lip. I didn't say a thing. Then I heard the sigh. I believed she was coming to her truth about not wanting this man as a life partner. I asked her not to answer right then, but to think some more and get back to me the next day.

I went back to the people responding to her dilemma on Facebook.

Melody: "That happened to me too. I was only married two years when he told me he wanted children. I was devastated. I divorced him. Now I'm with the most amazing man. It worked out for the best."

Another woman bravely shared this:

Phyliss: "I'm married a long time. We both felt sure we never wanted to be parents. Now, he says he changed his mind. I hope that my marriage can survive this. I love him dearly. I guess ultimately it boils down to if he can find fulfillment with me vs if he feels that only a kid can do that for him. I've never been interested in being any kind of a mom to humans. I refuse to ignore who I am at my core."

Whether to leave a relationship that gives you a lot of positive experiences is a tough call. Here's something to consider: if the partner you're with is wavering, try to find out what they feel is missing in the relationship. I once heard Laura Scott, author of *Two is Enough: A Couple's Guide To Living Childless by Choice*, say, "Many times, it's a need to nurture that's missing when a person feels they must have a child."

She was my guest speaker on one of the NOKID group cruises I host and plan. Laura was on that first group cruise. When one of the men mentioned his fear of missing something precious in life, she quietly got to his real need.

He wasn't saying much when we gathered in our private meeting room for sixteen people. It was the morning of our first day at sea, which meant no stopping at ports. I chose that time because I knew people wanted to have fun with the activities on the ship. Meeting early in the day gave us lots of time to play later.

He was the last to enter the room, and sat down at the far end of the long table nearest to the door. His wife sat next to him. Did he sit close to the door so he could leave quickly? He took the pitcher in front of him and poured himself a glass of water. He didn't look at ease. But many people are nervous meeting people for the first time. His chattier wife was speaking to another woman on her right.

She had a sun hat that she took off and placed on the back of her chair. Her bathing suit cover-up showed that she planned to go to the pool or perhaps the childfree deck to sunbathe. He wore Bermuda shorts with one of the Caribbean-themed shirts you see on lots of cruises. He had slightly receding salt-and-pepper hair. He sat back, folded his arms as if protecting us from him (or maybe himself from us), and sipped from his water glass.

After listening to a few of the common conversation starters—who we were, why we were there, and what we hoped to gain from this experience—he moved forward, placed his empty water glass on the table, and said, "Maybe I'm the only one here not totally sure of living the childfree lifestyle. I love helping people. As a parent, wouldn't I get to do that, on a very personal, fulfilling basis, every day?"

Immediately, a few people rolled their eyes or looked at each other with frowns. Then everyone seemed to look at Laura, as if to say, "Help!"

Laura responded with this eye-opener: "You're talking about the joys of nurturing. Can you think of ways you can nurture without raising a child?" She reminded us that to "nurture" means to help something grow and thrive.

That led us to share many possibilities for nurturing without becoming a parent.

1. Volunteering in many worthwhile organizations, with or without children.
2. Rescuing a pet.
3. Growing a garden.
4. Being a true and caring friend.
5. Nurturing your political choice by getting involved in your local political party.

I looked at the man who started this conversation with Laura. He wasn't conversing. The man sat without expression, his arms still folded in front of him, leaning back a little in his chair. Was he trying to get further away? Was he taking in the suggestions or privately thinking, *Is she kidding? Does she really think taking care of a garden is the same as nurturing a child?*

Sandy, a petite woman in her early thirties who already had a slightly sunburned nose, perhaps from the upper-deck bon voyage party as we left, offered this: "My husband joined the Big Brothers Big Sisters program, where a kid is paired up with an adult of the same gender. They get together one to two times per week to hang out. Yesterday, while I packed for this cruise, my husband took the kid on a nature hike. They've also done archery, gone bowling, gone to movies, did indoor rock climbing, visited a museum, et cetera. They're going to start volunteering at a food bank together after our cruise."

Another male cruiser laughed out loud, saying, "I like that. I think it's better than being a dad. You get to bring them back afterwards, right?"

That got a laugh from all of us. But not from the man who had stated his ambivalence.

After adding to her list with several more possibilities, Laura's last suggestion was the cherry on the hot fudge sundae: "One of the most beautiful ways of nurturing is nurturing your own self! Find the things you love doing. Then make plans to do them!"

This is when I saw that man, who'd seemed to want to leave from the minute he came in, bring his chair forward. Did Laura's words register? Had he ever thought about simply nurturing his own inner child as worthwhile and possibly rewarding? I never got to find out, because after that first meeting the man and his wife never joined us in any activities. I once saw his wife walking toward one of the onboard tax-free shops. Stopping her, I asked if everything was okay. She sighed, "I guess we still have a lot to think about. He doesn't want to hear any more." I never heard from either of them again.

And that's okay. There are many people who truly want children. We don't want to villainize anyone. It's their right. It's their life. It's their choice, as much as it is our choice to live a childfree lifestyle.

There's another group of people whose life partners swear they never want children and love the idea of the childfree lifestyle. However, they don't really mean it! These people may have personalities that make for chronic broken promises.

Anita: "I knew my boyfriend was on his second divorce when I met him. He swore he never wanted any kids. He lied. I had no idea he had an eight-year-old child from his first marriage. About a month after we announced our engagement to our parents, *surprise*: he tells me that he has a son who'll be arriving any day from Germany. We'll be raising his son together! At that time he began telling me he wanted more children! Needless to say, we broke up shortly afterward. Best decision I ever made!"

People who repeatedly break commitments and promises are not, in my opinion, good prospects for partners or friendships. They're exhausting. You can't rely on them. You never know when their comments are real, or they're just placating you for the moment. Sometimes those people can be in your family, causing toxic, hurtful, or inconsistent reactions.

Who would want to be partnered or in a relationship with a person like this?

Those who have been hurt or misled by promises not kept may feel the anguish of rejection. They may question why they weren't enough for their beloved. I suggest being truthful with yourself.

Is raising a child a deal-breaker, or can you see yourself as a parent? If it's the former, then run as fast as you can! You'll never convince anyone that parenting isn't the fun promulgated through pronatalism.

Anger over broken promises hurts deeply. This is especially true if you've been up-front and honest about not wanting to have or raise children. Remember that it's not about you. It's about those who broke their promises. Make a list of the happy moments you shared or what that relationship taught you. Then make a list of the negative things in your relationship. Burn the negative list and keep the positive list. You probably have reasons to celebrate some of those experiences. The lists can also help you to see if a breakup is a good choice! If the bad things far outweigh the good things, it can open your eyes to things you may not want to face.

I also suggest you take time to grieve or feel bad before or after any breakup. When life gives you bitter disappointments, take time to feel that sadness or betrayal. The hurt of betrayal, rejection, or broken promises may vibrate every now and then, but if you've cried the last tear and seen the joy in letting go, the pain goes away. It becomes acceptance.

I also know the value of talking with a close friend. This is the time they really count in your life. Make sure it's a special friend you trust. Talking helps you grieve.

Getting empathy makes you feel acknowledged.

Whatever you do, don't go near any social media to vent! Whatever we write in the moment stays on the Internet forever. Also, in the heat of anger or betrayal, your emotions are filled with negativity. Many people hate that. Others feed on it, aiming daggers back at you. You can be seen as the villain, depending on who's reading your post. Your ex may also read what you write. Do you want that?

I suggest getting involved in a new group of people or some passion or hobby you've put off. A change of your usual routines may help ease the pain of rejection or betrayal. Look for childfree groups on the Internet or local meetups (www.meetup.com). Or start your own group!

Remember, there's another choice you can make regarding broken promises. Take a "no-fault" stance. Your relationship didn't make it. Many don't, for a myriad of reasons. If you both decide there is no fault, that one person simply changed their mind, you can choose to celebrate the good things you once shared. Here's where knowing how to face rejection may help. Here's where books like *The Untethered Soul* by Michael Singer or *Wild Chickens and Petty Tyrants* by Dr. Arnie Kozak can help you be here now, not mired in the past or the future.

My final heartfelt recommendation is for you to move on. Don't fear finding yourself in similar circumstance that ends in a broken promise from a beloved. That makes you their victim forever. You may also want to consider taking a permanent position, via tubal ligation or vasectomy.

Broken promises are always upsetting. People change their minds! People lie! Consider agreeing to a legal prenuptial document clarifying what happens if one person decides they want kids while the other doesn't. This clearly states your preference, and the consequences if there's a change. If the agreement is broken or changed, leading to a breakup, a prenuptial can specify who gets the family pet, or how any money is divided. It makes for an easier breakup, if it comes to that.

That way, at the very start of any relationship, your position is known. Many people have told me that once they broke off a relationship in which their childfree stance was betrayed, their life was filled with joy. Many took a different path, leading them to the love of their lives.

Finally, I leave you with this thought: people will come in and out of your life. Some will be a gift to you. Others will let you down. Each experience can be a lesson, even if it feels like a failure. Promises may be broken. As painful as that may be, even a broken promise may teach you a valuable lesson and lead you to a better life.

Remember Anna? The woman who opened this chapter with her tearful questioning about a broken promise? I reached out to her the day after our Skype experience. She still didn't have any clarity, so I suggested she take some time. Six months later, she emailed me and told me she'd parted with her boyfriend. She felt wonderful in her career, got the promotion she was aiming for, and was now in a relationship in which both partners openly knew there weren't going to be children. He had a vasectomy!

Chapter 4
Rejection While Traveling

"The secret to change is to focus all of your energy, not on fighting the old, but on building the new."
—Dan Millman, *Way of the Peaceful Warrior*

"You can handle just about anything that comes at you out on the road with a believable grin, common sense and whiskey."
—Bill Murray

You get on a plane. You find your row and take your seat by the aisle. You start praying to yourself—and you're not religious! It's not the fear of flying. This may be worse. You start your mantra: "PLEASE! PLEASE! PLEASE! Don't let any parent with their child sit *near* me. Worse yet, please not *next* to me!" Anxiously, you watch as people trundle on board with their bored expressions, pushing or pulling their luggage, looking up at the rows, back to their ticket, trying to find their seat. The plane is getting close to full. So far, you're in luck. You've seen parents and kids up in the front rows. That's okay. You brought earplugs. You're halfway back in the plane, seated behind the wing, near that emergency door. (Okay. You may have a little fear of flying.)

Suddenly you see her. It's that poor woman walking behind the man wearing the cowboy hat and chewing gum. She's looking harried and overcome with stress while moving a piece of luggage ahead of her. You think, *Didn't they allow parents to board first?* Either this one didn't hear the boarding instructions or she arrived late.

On her hip, you see a wide-eyed infant sucking a pink pacifier. Then, it happens!

You hear, "Excuse me? I think this is my seat. Do you mind holding her for a second?"

Well, what were you thinking? you lamely think to yourself. *Two empty seats next to you and you really thought she would be walking past them?* Many thoughts flood your head. You scan those sitting near you, who seem to be focused on what you'll do or say next. Is there another parent sitting nearby with their child on their lap? Would they mind changing *their* seat? Should you start to whimper and say you feel awful, but you have a fear of children? Dare you admit you're childfree by choice and would prefer not to hold their child or, even worse, sit near them?

"Sure," you say, wearing a false smile, trying to be a nice human. You think to yourself, *Maybe this one will be that ideal child.*

The minute you hold the child, who, judging by the pungent aroma assailing your nostrils, definitely needs a diaper change, the child starts screaming!

No, it's not a nightmare. It's a scenario many of us have experienced when flying. You start to wonder what you can do to get out of this situation. Any flight, no matter how long or short, can be a flight to hell when a child is screaming, fussing, or in need of attention. Those of us who chose a childfree lifestyle aren't "free" here! What's worse? We can't go anywhere to escape.

Here's what goes through my mind in these situations:

I can go to the back, find the attendant, and tell them my truths, and ask if *they* know of anyone who wouldn't mind switching with me. Maybe some parents without their kids? Or grandparent types who like children? But many of these adults are on vacation. They seek peace and quiet from their own daily, all-consuming parenting or grandparenting responsibilities. They may be the ones looking at their iPad and avoiding eye contact. So I think:

1. I can bite the bullet and try to help this fellow human.

2. I can truthfully say, "I'm sorry, I don't want to hold your baby or sit next to you."

Truth be told, both 1 and 2 feel uncomfortable for most childfree-by-choice people. There are some who love helping their nieces or nephews, or who have professions in which helping children is part of the fun. They may choose No 1. Of course, No. 2 would be overheard by too many people nearby, and not taken kindly by many. The verbal ridicule or evil stares of rejection would probably be catastrophic. You may even imagine yourself on a YouTube video with tons of comments about how awful you are.

I myself prefer not helping or being next to (or near) children. I know how difficult it may be for children to travel a long distance seated in an airplane. As a fearful flyer, I need as much peace and quiet as I can get to meditate and practice deep-breathing exercises. I may add, "I'm so sorry. I may have a little stomach challenge and need to get to the bathroom. I'm sure I'm not contagious! It's the effects of chemo!" (That really happens to me from time to time!)

This is just one scenario the childfree face over and over again while traveling. If we dare to tell our truths or hint in any way, shape, or form that we don't want to help a parent flying with an infant, we're considered lower than a snail at the bottom of the ocean. There are times we will gladly do what we can. However, many times we simply don't want to help.

I've had many people come to my support sites on Facebook complaining of children repeatedly kicking their seats on a plane. Or singing "Twinkle, Twinkle, Little Star" at the top of their lungs. Others may smile and find it adorable. I don't! I simply want to sit back, relax, and hope for a smooth flight with few distractions other than a bag of peanuts or pretzels and a drink to accompany the long hours.

Once, I had a small child tapping me on the head, saying "Hi!" I didn't answer. He repeated the tapping, saying "Hi" louder! I heard the clipped tone of annoyance from the parent: "The lady doesn't want to talk with you, honey!" And that's a nicer reaction than I would have gotten if I'd turned around to ask the parent to please stop their child from tapping me on the head. It could lead to ugly words between us. I know, because I once had the courage to gently ask if a child kicking the back of my seat could be told to stop. "Oh! You must one of those child-haters," the mother snapped."

"Actually, no! I'm a devoted teacher," I defiantly answered. "But I also want a peaceful flight!" Nothing changed. The child finally stopped and fell asleep. That's why I never said anything about the tapping on my head. I simply moved out of the child's reach until he gave up.

The rejection that many receive if they ask for parental control of an annoying child on a plane, train, or bus is frequently experienced. Sometimes, we don't dare say a word and suffer in silence. We know what we're up against! Sometimes, there's nothing anyone can do, especially if the child is having ear issues or otherwise not feeling well.

Once, on a very long flight, I sat in front of a little boy. It was a bumpy trip, with numerous storms and air pockets making me nervous. I wasn't a happy traveler. I kept looking at my watch, not believing only ten minutes had gone by when I was hoping for two hours. Suddenly, I heard the distinctive sounds of a person about to throw up. He sat behind me. Yes. That little boy was projectile vomiting! I felt badly for him and his mom. I felt worse for me, as it poured onto my armrest. Now, I'm not sure if a parent would be as upset as I was. I can only think it wouldn't be as bad for them. For me, it was awful. The attendant came running down the aisle with coffee grounds and quickly spread them to "stop the smell," as she told me. But the lingering medicinal odor of the Clorox cleaning wipe mixed with a hint of vomit and coffee grounds didn't make for a terrific flight. I looked at my watch and sighed. Another six hours to go.

That's why, on many childfree support sites on Facebook, people are asking for childfree flights. And some airlines are listening. The budget airline in India, IndiGo Airlines, launched childfree zones that ban children under twelve from the first eight rows. It's only eight rows, but it's a start! An article on the initiative generated comments of outrage. One comment was: "Parents fear other airlines may do the same." Seriously? Why do eight rows on a large plane make parents fear anything?

The Singapore-based airline Scoot offers a chance to pay extra for seats away from children. When I asked my followers on Facebook if they would pay extra for that distance, the answer was a resounding "Yes!"

Both Malaysia Airlines and AirAsia also offer childfree zones or special offers for passengers seeking a childfree zone.

Not one U.S. airline I researched, to date, has made any childfree offers or childfree zones available.

Here's a list of airlines I would stay away from if possible. They're very child-and-family-centered:

Virgin Atlantic: Preboarding and children's menus.

Jet Blue: Preboarding and unlimited juice and snacks for children under two.

Emirates Airlines: Their motto is "Family Comes First." They provide preboarding, a kid's pack filled with fun activities, and an eye mask for kids. (An eye mask for kids? You read that right.)

Asiana: Preboarding. Expectant mothers get a cart so they don't have to walk to the plane. Asiana boasts of its "expectant mothers care." Children get magic shows, face painting, and cookie-baking class on board.

Qantas: Offers a family zone preboarding area with Sony PlayStations, toys, books, and free refreshments for children and parents. Onboard, children get in-flight child-centered entertainment and activity packs.

Of course, some may argue that giving this much attention to children makes them less bored. Nevertheless, small children are difficult to sit near. No amount of eye masks, baking, or face painting will help a fussy child.

If flights were opened to serve a growing number of childfree frequent flyers looking for a more pleasant and less stressful experience, who would suffer? Businesspeople would be able to focus on their work in-flight. People going to a vacation could enjoy watching a movie or listening to music without the primal screams of a child in need. (By the way, many parents would like this, too!) Those traveling with little ones can help each other if they sit near each other. Those traveling without their children would get a head start on their long-awaited and much-needed vacation—in peace.

I asked some of my Facebook followers to share their experiences with rejection while traveling. Here are a few of their responses:

"I really get sick and tired of having no room to store my carry-ons because parents put their strollers and diaper bags and whatever into the overhead compartments. Allowing this rejects my things as being less important [than] parents' overhead needs. The last four trips I took, I had luggage in my lap and under my seat. It wasn't stuff I wanted to check because it was fragile equipment. I'm sure the FAA probably wouldn't agree with this. And of course, the flight attendants don't respond kindly when you ask why parents can't stow their strollers elsewhere. We're given the hint of their rejecting feelings that we're against parental needs through their rolled eyes or sighs."

"I hate it when parents buy one early boarding pass on Southwest Airlines and then save seats for their family of 5 who wait in the other lines because they didn't pay the extra fees. I find myself in a controlled rage that forces me to sit in one of those saved seats whether I want that seat or not. They can rant and rave and give me the evil stares begging for their family to sit together. Not happening! The entitlement of parents is what gets me the most!"

Another mode of transportation aiming rejection arrows at the childfree is the subway or bus services in cities. It's been a while since I used these methods of travel.

Born and raised in New York City, I can remember many trips on subways and buses. The crowds are awful. The available seats can't accommodate the masses using this form of transportation. Truthfully, I don't miss the experience!

I repeatedly hear indignation over a scenario in which a pregnant woman will board a subway or bus and stare at people who aren't giving up a seat for them. People sitting near those not giving up their seats deliver stares of rejection. Behind those cold, glaring eyes, they may be thinking, *How rude! Look at that poor pregnant woman. Why can't they give up a seat! They're selfish!* However, they don't give up their own seat.

Before anyone suggests we're cold-hearted, hear me out. Of course, if we can give up a seat and don't mind, that's fine. But how many childfree people really need that seat, too? We have many men and women suffering from silent illnesses such as fibromyalgia or severe back pain. Standing, for them, can be just as bad as for any pregnant woman. It's not that one is better or worse than the other. Pregnancy is a chosen lifestyle for most. Shouldn't the realities women may face on any mode of transportation be understood before they choose them? But pregnancy is regarded with awe and delight. It's a time when a lot of attention is given to the pregnant woman. To withhold that attention comes as a shock to the pregnant woman, and to anyone watching.

One of the perks of being childfree is the number of options that childlessness creates for travel. That's not saying we can all travel whenever we like. It's a myth to picture all of us lolling on a Caribbean beach or taking off on a whim to visit all the countries on our bucket lists.

Many people without children face harsh challenges with money, jobs, or health. Many can't afford a lot of traveling.

For those of us who have saved some money and have the time, traveling can be joyful. However, there are a few things we want as childfree people. We don't enjoy being around children all the time. Picture this: you check into your lovely hotel and head for the gorgeous pool with the bar where you can sit in the warm, azure water. First, you get a lounge chair, place a towel on it, and relax, sipping your mojito. Life is good... until you hear "CANONBALL!" as a child jumps into the pool. The water splashes over you like a giant tsunami. There are shrieks of laughter. You're not laughing. You checked, and this was labeled as an adult pool. Why is that kid there? You seek out the parent, who's lamely saying, "Honey! Don't do that!" However, the child can't even hear, as he's getting ready to jump again. You smile your nicest fake smile, reminding the parent of the "adults only" sign. "What's the matter? Don't like kids?" you hear as a cold scowl is aimed at you. You want to defend your right to the area specifically labeled "adults only."

If we suggest they move to the child's pool area, we may hear, "But I want to enjoy this vacation, too. The bar is here! The kids' pool is too far." We think, *You chose to be a parent! There are rules here.* We can never utter that thought, because it would evoke defensive anger. It's as if, for some parents, the childfree have no wants or needs that come close to those of a parent. You move to another area, filled with frustration, knowing you can't reach that parent.

This is why many adults-only hotels and vacation properties are popular among childfree people. Many are also all-inclusive, where drinks, food, entertainment, and lodging are provided for one bundled price. However, the limited number of adults-only hotels don't come close to providing adequate options for the childfree traveler.

Hotel pools aren't the only challenge faced by traveling childfree adults. Lodging and dining issues challenge the childfree time and time again. I often think, *Is this rejection, or failure to acknowledge the legitimate needs of people who don't have children? Are the needs of children and their parents always more important than the needs of those who don't procreate or raise children?* I wonder!

Kids on vacation seem to be overly loud and happy. Of course they are. We were once kids, and those of us whose parents could afford to travel remember the delight of those new experiences. Except that kids never think whether running up and down hotel corridors or slamming doors in excitement is acceptable. Sometimes, you can hear them stomping on the floor above your head as they jump off of beds or play tag in their rooms. Or they want to hear their cartoons at high volume when they're next door. Or they may have a meltdown because they weren't allowed to go to the pool after dinner. Or they have sibling rivalry and scream about how they hate their brother or sister.

It's not the kid's fault! Too many parents want to be their child's friend, and so fail to teach boundaries with consequences. If we dare to question their child's behavior or ask for help from the parent, we get the rejected shrug, or worse yet, "Don't tell me how to raise my kid!" If we call the front desk, we're up against the possibility that the staff are also parents and have no sympathy for us cold-hearted non-parents. I suggest another possibility:

designate certain hotel floors and rooms childfree or adults-only.

As with any hotel or restaurant experience while traveling, there's nothing wrong with asking if there's a childfree area the minute you enter the facility, or even while making the reservation. (Of course, if you're in a Disney park, don't even think about that!)

Recently, we went on a car trip to visit dear friends in Georgia. We stopped for breakfast at a well-known chain restaurant facing a main road. There was a booth near our booth with two women and three children. Two little identical twin girls were seated. An infant sat in a high chair. I noticed the mothers had purchased the children doughnuts with sprinkles. Of course that would mean sugar highs! The twins sat looking out the window behind them, munching on those doughnuts, counting: "I see one blue car! I see two black cars." With each sighting, they got louder and louder with the excitement of the game. One mom said, "Shhhh! Not so loud!" That "Shhhh" wasn't even acknowledged by the twins, and the mom continued to chat with the other woman.

I looked around for another table, but there wasn't one. I would never ask that mom to quiet the escalating piercing screams of her children, because I know from past experience that I would get, "Don't tell me how to parent my children!" The rejection would be loud and clear. Or I might hear, "How about overlooking it? It's just two little girls having fun." You can't win.

One of my Facebook followers, a woman from India, posted the following when I asked about experiences of rejection while traveling:

"Well, not rejected directly, but definitely missed

advantages provided to parents. Many resorts have larger rooms reserved for families. Since we're only two, we're offered smaller units! By the way, the costs are the same! If we asked for the larger unit, we were told they're reserved only for families. I said, "I'm a family of two!" The hotel clerk looked at me, mouth opened, eyebrows crunched together in shock, and sighed heavily, saying, "Sorry. I mean a family with children!"

An ardent camping devotee in the U.S. posted this response:

"Then, there are those campgrounds. It's almost as if the people using camping for vacations are only thought to be parents. Not so! Yet, why do many campsites charge for two adults and two kids? However, if you're three adults traveling together, without children, they'll charge you for an "extra person." It's the same space in the dirt! Seriously? Maybe that's why childfree adults are tired of this rejection and discrimination and seek out a growing number of adult-only campsites?"

If you're planning to take off from work for a vacation during any school vacation time, you may not get your first choice. I hear many stories about getting the side-eyed glance when asking for travel time during school vacations. If parents ask for the same time, while their kids *aren't* in school, the person without a child may not get their first choice. Parents' needs come first in planning travel or vacations with their children. It's a form of rejection. One lifestyle is deemed more important than the other.

Rejection is a challenge we may face for simply choosing an alternative lifestyle. Most parents will think it's trivial for us to complain about our challenges while traveling. They think we're silly to make a big deal about childfree flights, lodging, or areas in restaurants. Not to give up a seat to a pregnant woman on a bus or train is deemed rude or in bad taste. Our displeasure when posted rules aren't followed appears discriminatory toward their children. It's frustrating when our first choices for vacation time aren't honored because a parent requested the same week off. Having to pay more for an extra adult at a campground is truly unfair when a family of four gets in cheaper.

But think carefully. No matter what rejections you face while traveling, you never have to hear "Are we there yet?" You don't have to worry that your kids will be bored if there's no pool at your hotel. You don't have to spend time at a washing machine because your infant pooped in his romper. You don't have to argue with your child because they want Froot Loops at dinner and you chose a nice restaurant.

Remember this: travel always has challenges. You don't have to be a victim of rejection or favoritism toward parents. Remember to speak up if you want a childfree dining area. It's okay to remind parents that an adult pool is for the needs of people who aren't traveling with children. You can always move if an unruly child or a parent who doesn't care about following rules is bothering you. If you're in a hotel with screaming children or kids running up and down the halls, call the front desk and ask for help. All travel agents can book adult vacations. Many airlines are now hearing the requests for childfree zones. Write and ask for them. Insist on a childfree cruise—they do exist, but you'll have to pay double. If seated on a plane near a child who is having a meltdown, you can ask to change your seat. If that's not possible, always make sure you've brought earplugs or headphones to drown out the noise. As for giving up your seat for pregnant women, do it if you want. If you are suffering from a physical challenge, not feeling well, or simply want to stay in your seat, you have that right.

You're childfree by choice. Even these negative experiences can be of value, as you see what parents go through when they travel with their kids. It can make you feel lucky to be childfree by choice. Travel is still an awesome experience, rejections or not!

Chapter 5
Rejection in the Workplace

"Coming together is a beginning. Keeping together is progress. Working together is success."
—Edward Everett Hale

Most of us have to work for a living, unless some wealthy relative leaves us a bundle in their will or we win the lottery. In our dreams! So, we choose a career or job that floats our personal boat. Sometimes it's a good fit. Other times, we accept the fact that it brings us needed money and wait for the clock to tell us we can go home.

Our personal lifestyle choices shouldn't affect anyone but ourselves in the workplace. However, many childfree people find their work experiences are tarnished if they mention they never want to have or raise children. This is also true for anyone who faces infertility, then changes from identifying as childless to childfree. There is a huge difference between those words, at work and in life. Childlessness is perceived as a sad, barren experience. Childfree is considered a selfish word, with a hint of regret to come once it's too late to have children.

Many childless people face rejection at work. They're endlessly told of yet another infertility center, adoption agency, or successful surrogacy story. Although people making those suggestions see them as helpful, infertile people feel they're facing rejection by their bodies yet again, or social rejection of them personally.

In this chapter, we'll explore the often-surprising experience of being childfree in the workplace. It may be shocking to learn what many childfree people endure. To those who know it's not shocking, it will validate your own feelings toward rejection in your work environment. It may spur you on to tell your truths, or keep you quiet to avoid the negative effects of rejection. I'll share interviews with people, research, and my own experiences as a childfree woman.

I always loved my chosen career. Teaching was the perfect profession for me. Seeing those aha moments in students' faces encouraged me to do more. I felt hungry to start a new day and get to work. Even when snow covered the ground and my car had to be de-iced before the sun rose, I looked forward to getting to school. Being in my student's lives made me feel contented, nourished, and happy.

My workplaces during my last ten years of teaching were two schools: Parkway Elementary and Woodland Middle School in East Meadow on Long Island, New York. It was a daunting task to teach kindergarten through eighth grade. I wore two distinct hats. One was for the little guys who sat looking at me with their deer-in-the-headlights stares. They left their countries, families, friends, pets, foods, and customs to come to a strange country where they had no clue what was being said. For me, that meant thinking every day about how I could make language comprehensible. How could I make them less fearful of attempting a new language?

My peers saw me carrying in objects for activities to help the children understand the words I was teaching by doing, holding, hearing, and seeing. Once, I learned the hard way that bringing in fall leaves gathered from my backyard to teach kindergarteners about colors, counting, and comparison wasn't such a good idea. Although they got to produce the words "red," "green," "yellow," "big," "little," and numbers one through five, the custodian was livid the next day. Those leaves I brought in a large plastic bag also carried ants!

After leaving the little ones, I put on my second hat and went to the middle school, where I met my ESL pre-teens, the ones with raging hormones, acne, and the angst of trying to fit in. Too often they faced the awful reality of rejection through prejudice. Other students made fun of their accents. Sometimes, they were mocked at lunch for their foods, with their strange smells of curry, garlic, or other unknown, pungent odors lingering on their clothes. Often they were laughed at for wearing the same clothes they had grown up wearing with pride. In East Meadow, a hijab covering a religious girl's hair and the traditional shalwar kameez shirt for boys and girls didn't fit in.

Every year, around Martin Luther King's birthday, my middle school students prepared "Speeches From Their Hearts." Learning how to write and deliver a speech in English to inspire, educate, and get more friends was the goal. They would speak to three or four classes at a time from a stage. Their peers would hear what they'd been through, leaving their countries and trying to fit in. It always ended the same way; tears on the faces of the students and their teachers. Sometimes, genuine friendships were made after such raw realities were shared.

My students knew I cared deeply. It wasn't only about learning English. I often went to their teachers and tried to offer simple ways of helping their ESL students. After a while, I begged the guidance department not to place students in classes that I knew would be a waste of their time. Rejection and prejudice exist among teachers as well. I know! You may find that shocking. I faced teachers who made no excuses for not wanting to help my students. I would hear, "Hey Marcia! You go home without another job of raising kids! I go home to my family! I don't have time to prepare the extra lessons or worksheets that can reach your kids. I don't have that time!" I couldn't argue or say, "That's what you're being paid for!"

The parents of my students knew I cared, too. I took the extra time I had (without being paid extra) to call them if I felt something needed to be discussed. Sometimes, it was to sing praises of how hard their children worked. Often, I would make appointments to visit their homes. My husband and I enjoyed meals with my students and their families. In my last ten years of teaching, that could mean exotic foods from other cultures. We tasted curry dishes, enjoyed roti, and tried foods I never knew how to cook. We could do this because we had the time. We had no children at home to care for.

Not one of my ESL students or their parents during my last ten years of teaching had any issues with my not having children of my own. It never came up in conversations. It was probably considered too private to discuss in the cultures of my international families.

However, I once faced an irate group of teachers when I suggested that running around the school with hard-boiled eggs in a basket wasn't the best way to teach what it means to be a responsible parent. When I suggested a programmed doll that would cry in the night unless it was held, I heard snide comments: "We know you don't want kids, Marcia. We don't want to turn them off completely!"

The ignorant comments made me pause. I didn't want

to make waves, as I'd suffered too many years of being blacklisted from teaching after being on *60 Minutes* in 1974. Now it was 1990. I was back into teaching, with a new name and a new subject, ESL. I still feared being falsely labeled as disliking children or trying to discourage my students from having kids. When the topic of kids was raised in my first year back to teaching, I honestly replied, "I don't have any. My school kids are the ones I want, not biological kids." I know! I walked a fine line between being shunned and expressing pride in the childfree lifestyle.

All I said to those teachers was that in my opinion, child care should not taught by forcing kids to carry hard-boiled eggs. If the eggs fell, it was "egg abuse." If the kids had things to do, they had to get an "egg sitter" to sign their egg sitter sheet. One of my students, after this nonsense was over, left his egg in his locker before the Easter/Passover week off. Needless to say, the school had to be fumigated for the rotten egg smell assailing everyone's nostrils. The student's comment was, "Mrs. Davis, I forgot!" Quietly, I asked him how he felt about the responsibility of having an egg baby. He sighed and said, "Well, men don't care for real kids. Women do!" He was from Pakistan.

The teachers' lounge is a place where many teachers eat lunch with their peers. I knew the importance of connection with my peers. In any work environment, working in harmony with others helps everyone. However, it got to be very, very challenging.

Many times, along with endless talk about students, there was even more chatter about the teachers' children at home. I totally got that. When you're a parent, there's a need to share, learn, and tell stories about your children's experiences. It's part of parents' lives.

For me, and for so many people venting on my Facebook sites about staff dining rooms, it got old. Frankly, many people get tired of hearing stories about co-workers' kids. We have no connection to those stories, brags, rants, or requests for support. Childfree people aren't cold-hearted! But why would I want to hear about little Marissa's teething or sweet Johnny's first baseball game? Could I eat my lunch without all the stories from proud parents? If I tried to change the topic or mentioned planning for a trip or looking to buy a piano and asking for advice, I'd see the rolled eyes or hear, "We don't have the time or money for those things. We're busy raising children." One of my followers said she got tired when she heard, "When are *you* going to settle down?"

I once ventured a suggestion to help an irate teacher facing her son's hellish teenage years, only to hear, "Marcia! You never had kids! How could you know?" I couldn't win.

So, I retreated to my room, hid in a corner where they couldn't see me, locked the door, played classical music, and enjoyed a quiet lunch.

Other childfree people have shared on Facebook how they take to going out for lunch, or eating alone at their desks, to avoid child-centered discussions.

Even before my TV exposure in 1974, my first year of teaching elementary school, in 1964, in PS 113 Manhattan, resulted in rejection in the workplace. I didn't even know what the word "pronatalism" meant then!

Fernando Munez was the exemplary child in my second-grade class. He was well-mannered, crossed himself before eating any food, and did his best to learn. I wasn't trained in ESL at that time. My father was. He gave me some pointers about reaching this bilingual child. I loved that little boy. However, slowly, I noticed a dramatic change. He became sullen, defiant, not doing his homework, laughing while I taught, talking when he shouldn't. His good grades started to slide precipitously. I was stumped! I suspected he wanted to be accepted but had chosen a group of rowdy kids. I called his mom and arranged for a conference before class started.

She came into my classroom before the children arrived. I mentioned how much I loved her son. I related in simple English how well he had begun in my class. She beamed with pride. Then I got to the reason for my concern. Her whole demeanor changed. She asked me if I had children. I didn't. I was just married, and didn't know for sure that I would be childfree by choice back then. I distinctly remember her rising from her chair and saying, "You have no kids. How can you tell me about my boy? He's just being a boy! But you wouldn't know! When you have kids, you'll understand."

There it was. She thought I hated her child and had no ability to help him because I didn't have kids of my own. I wanted to help him, but she wouldn't accept that I might be able to, simply because I wasn't a parent.

I've heard this challenge recounted many times by other childfree teachers. It's almost laughable when you think of the required training we endure throughout our careers. It's not just about the academics. It's about the many modalities of reaching children, behavioral issues, and how to overcome them by setting boundaries and enforcing consistent consequences. I could have helped Mrs. Munez. However, I was deemed not to have the abilities of a parent, therefore, any suggestion from me fell on deaf ears.

Some of the most annoying things the childfree face in the workplace are erroneous conclusions concerning our work-life balance. Nothing compares to taking care of children in free time. If the childfree dare to talk about their need for alone time, or time to help aging parents or sick pets, it pales in comparison to taking care of a child. In fact, too often the childfree are expected to pick up parents' slack, without extra pay. If parents are called home to care for a sick child or take a child to a scheduled doctor visit, many employers think it's perfectly okay to ask non-parents to pitch in for them and do extra work.

Too often, non-parents aren't compensated. Yet, if they dare ask their bosses to go home a little earlier because a dog is ready to come home from the vet and they'll be closed by the time they get off work, it's considered trivial. "Can't you get another person to pick that dog up?" is often heard, as related to me by my followers on the Internet. Or they're told they can leave, but they'll be docked for the time off. The bottom line is that childfree people often feel their employers don't value their work-life balance as much as they value that of parents.

Many childfree people go to their workplace every morning and return home to a quiet environment (unless they have pets, like my snarky rescue Chihuahua). They sit down, breathe deeply, relax, or have a glass of wine. Some enjoy cooking dinner. Others go out to eat. A few pick up their phones and place a take-out or delivery order. Many are busy after work doing errands we all have to do: grocery shopping, picking up clothes at the dry cleaners, dentist appointments, or visiting the gym. Some go home and volunteer with Meals on Wheels, or mentor kids at risk.

In her revealing article "The Brutal Truth About Being Childless at Work" (Nov. 07, 2015, *Fortune* magazine), Laura Carroll suggests that workplace culture values caring for children more than anything else an employee can do outside of work. Anything that non-parents do can't compare to the endless commitments of parenting. She writes, "Whether childfree or childless, we still have a ways to go when it comes to society accepting those with no children without judgment or stigma."

As you read the following remarks from my Facebook followers, you'll see how Carroll's suggestion vibrates in the hearts of childfree people experiencing rejection in the workplace. Here are a few of their heartfelt posts.

Sherri: "I feel angry being childfree at work. When I'm asked to work evenings, weekends, and holidays because people with kids 'need' time off, it gets old. When people with kids come to me and ask me to cover their shift because they had to do something with their kid, I want to scream. Never mind the fact that I haven't had a weekend off in over a month. No! Their time is *more* valuable than mine because they couldn't figure out how birth control works."

I feel Sherri's anger. Not having a weekend off in over a month simply because she's childfree is unconscionable. Yet, who can she complain to? Are her needs considered equal to those of parents? Probably not.

Jenn: "At my work I've been asked a few times when I'll have kids. When I say I'm not interested I hear, 'Oh you gotta have one.' Mind you, these are people whose grown kids hate them. I hear their sob stories all the time during lunch."

But if Jenn dared to mention that one of the reasons she chose never to have children was because of common parent-child conflicts, she would be given the evil eye.

Phoung: "People know I don't want any kids. If they ask me why and get upset about it, I tell them I would rather buy a house and retire early. That usually shuts them up. But, all day, I can feel their anger. Are they jealous? It doesn't make for a pleasant work experience. I try to ignore them."

I would guess everyone wants to get along with his or her peers at work. Maybe some people couldn't care less? That's okay, too. Anger over a personal choice affecting no one but the person making the choice is beyond reason. In this situation, Phoung has two choices: ignore the rebuff, or face it with dignity and try to make clear that it's not welcomed.

Carlos: "I'm defensive if it's assumed I'll be there every holiday because I don't have kids. Screw that. I have a family. It's my wife and pets... not to mention a sick dad in need of a ride to his physical therapy, or my sister asking for help with her kids after school. I also have hobbies. My time off is equally important. Or is it?"

Is it? Not according to Carroll's research, and not according to what I've heard from too many people who write to me every day. (By the way, I love how Carlos defines his family.) It's upsetting to know that his personal struggle with his dad isn't given equal consideration to the needs of parents and children. Time off is something we all treasure and count on to make our lives more enjoyable. Why should it be different for the childfree?

Nala: "Nope. No problems for me at work. I'd tell them to shove it. If there is a day I think parents got priority over me, I just won't request off. I'd call out sick. But that doesn't seem to be an issue... this far."

I'm happy for Nala. I also know her personally, and can't imagine anyone taking advantage of this powerfully strong woman on any level. I'm hoping her share helps others to find their courage to step up for their own wants and needs.

April: "Next week, April 27th is 'Bring Your Sons/Daughters to Work Day.' My workplace participates in this. In the morning, the kids get to do different activities, but in the afternoon they're dumped off to their parents. Which means a bunch of little people roaming around my office. As part of the administrative assistant team, there's no doubt I'll get called to either take pictures or help the kids find their parents. It's no coincidence that I'm taking a personal day that day! Leave me out of that mess."

I believe April was proactive. Her personal day off was the right choice. Why suffer and be a smiling helper when it truly would upset her?

John: "Because I have no kids, it's expected that my career is everything. My manager thinks I'm in need of climbing that corporate ladder. Truth is... it's not my priority. I love my work. But, I love going home more. It's my oasis. I'm also active, involved with teaching illiterates to read in our library. I get tired of hearing, 'You know? If you want to get to the top, you should do more here!'"

Of the many shares, this one by John caught my eye. Isn't it fascinating to think his comment may be true? Just because we don't have children doesn't necessarily mean we want to climb the corporate latter to the top. Many of us enjoy our lifestyle and want to get back into the opportunities afforded by not raising children. Our hearts aren't always attached to career goals. It's an assumption, isn't it?

Al: "When a male sales manager asked if I had kids, at first I politely said, 'No.' After repeated questions over the next few months, I finally told him we chose not to have kids. He proceeded to give me a long speech and say that people have motivators in life. He found having a family the biggest motivator for his salesmen, and said that I should seriously reconsider."

I wrote Al a private message asking how he felt about this. Al admitted he was upset, then angry. Basically, his manager wanted his salesmen to have kids because he feels they'll try harder to take home more money for the endless needs of children. Even though Al's sales were constantly high, he was given that pronatalistic bullshit speech.

I felt truly upset, until he told me he didn't work there anymore. He left and found a better position with a manager who never gave him sermons about having children.

When I was blacklisted from teaching, I started my own direct mail business. A few salespeople were needed. My business succeeded because I trained my salespeople to show honesty and integrity and never to lie. If a sales force is working only to make money for their kids, they can lie for sales. If you have a sales force that believes in their product, that belief shines through and results in more sales. I'm thrilled Al found another position where he is honored for his sales, not for procreating.

Angela: "When asked if we have kids yet or how many kids we have, I reply, 'None! We have no intentions to ever have them.' People usually follow-up asking what my husband thinks of that, or saying, 'Just wait until he changes your mind!' I always answer that if we didn't agree on not having children before we married, we never would have married."

Steven: "At work, I was asked if I'm having kids. I replied, 'I hate kids' and was basically shown the door. It worked out because I found another job where nobody cared if I had or didn't have kids!"

Courtney: "I was ostracized at my workplace for not chipping in money I didn't have for a co-worker's baby shower. I feel if you don't earn enough money to get what you need for any child, don't get pregnant. It was women co-workers who made a fuss. I didn't hear from any male, although I think they secretly envied me for not giving in to the bullshit."

Christopher: "I haven't had any outright rejection—that would potentially open employers to legal action and they know it. The discrimination I've experienced is more subtle, more akin to 'social exclusion' because I don't participate in the kiddie cult. I've been subjected to rude comments like, 'What's the purpose of your marriage if you're not having children?' And, 'What DOES your wife DO with all her time?' The implication being that we're somehow lacking, morally or ethically, and therefore unworthy of regard, consideration or trust. It's difficult to find friendships with this reaction."

Although Christopher says he hasn't felt rejection specifically pertaining to his job, social rejection is never a pleasant experience. It's still rejection. I hope that after he reads this book, he'll find the pride to tell these people how insulting they are by explaining to them that they're just reacting to the myths they've been taught. Just because he and his wife are childfree by choice doesn't mean they have endless hours of freedom. Many childfree people are quite involved with their extended families and communities, or simply enjoy their alone time. There's nothing wrong with that. It's part of why people love going home after a hard day at work. Their childfree lifestyle offers endless possibilities.

I personally answered every comment sent to me in private messages on Facebook, suggesting that pronatalism was at work. Each and every one, after emailing me, realized they were at fault for avoiding this topic. I encouraged them to share their feelings and ask their bosses or managers to understand the needs and wants of non-parents. Every person was delighted to see they were heard! No longer were they expected to stay late or take over the work of a parent forced to run home to some crisis. They didn't have to listen to endless kid-centered stories at work or donate to baby showers, because their bosses began respecting those who don't want, can't have, or shouldn't have children.

That's a lie. It never happened that way. It happens in my dreams, or when I think of a world where parents are considered equivalent to all the non-parents on this planet. It's a dream of people being rational in a baby-centric world that esteems parents while the childfree are considered second-class citizens.

However, it could be a reality, not just a dream, if we step up to the plate. From the ether of a thought can come concrete, positive results. We can start by valuing and sharing our needs. No manager, boss, or co-worker can read our mind. But play the game to win. If you complain or whine, you'll get nowhere, and you may lose your job. (Which, as you've read, may not be so bad!) If you start by asking for help and sharing your fear of what others may think, you place your manager, boss, or co-workers in a listening mode, not a defensive one.

Tell your truths. Share how unfair it feels to be burdened with extra work when a parent must leave early to tend for a child. If *you* must leave early, ask for rational compassion.

Your requests aren't more or less valid than any other person's, regardless of whether or not they have children. Accommodation should be granted based on need, and whether others can take over your work without being unduly inconvenienced.

There's some good news. More people are saying their bosses prefer hiring the childfree by choice! Legally, employers can't ask whether you have a child or plan to have children, but you can be loud and proud in sharing your lifestyle. You won't have to be running home for child emergencies, parent-teacher meetings, or school plays. Many employees regard childfree women as more committed to their careers. Perhaps this is reverse pronatalism?

The "family man" ranks high in social approval and is rewarded with accolades at work. A father is seen as responsible. He's working hard to make money for his family. A mother is seen as too consumed with her children to give her work the attention it deserves. A non-parent is seen as the one to step in to pick up their slack. It's terribly unfair and wrong. It's labeling without rational thinking. I found a Reddit post illustrating irrational thinking when it comes to mothers who feel they offer more than non-parents. It's from a male boss interviewing a potential female employee:

"I'm an employer. Yesterday I had some job interviews with potential employees. One of them was a woman who put her motherhood above anything else. My question — What's your greatest achievement? This woman — My children! Me — No, no, I mean professionally. She — That's not important, because if a woman is a mother, she's able to do any job, and if a woman is not a mother, she's not as valuable.

I've heard many interesting answers in interviews, but this was the first time I heard something like this. I asked her some more questions to clarify her suitability to be an employee and every one of her answers had 'because I'm a mother' in it.

Well, needless to say, she's not getting a call back. And not because she's a mother, but because she didn't actually answer any of my questions and basically stated that I should hire her only because she's a mother."

It's time we speak up when facing unfair expectations of childfree people in the workplace. We, the childfree, have every right to enjoy our private time. Even if we're running home to a hobby, friends, a good book, a run, walking our dog, or a dinner out by ourselves, these experiences are as valuable as any experience a parent looks forward to. We need to share our feelings about our hours, expectations, and, if necessary, being taken advantage of or rejected by others with our managers. We need to challenge the assumption that a non-parent's home life isn't as important as raising children. The facts are far from the myths. The facts support the reality that many non-parents have just as many responsibilities and joys (and challenges) to look forward to after work as their parent counterparts.

Feeling valued and respected is a necessity to anyone at work, whether they're parents or not. We should all ask ourselves: "Is my work done? Can it wait until tomorrow? Is it fair to ask a co-worker to take over my work knowing they're not getting extra pay?"

Do we have the courage to feel we have the right to tell parents we aren't responsible for their work-life balance or their parental responsibilities?

In my opinion, the childfree are no better or worse than parents in the workplace. We're all humans, working for a living. If we all recognize the importance of working together and respecting individual lifestyles without assuming that one is more important than the other, everyone wins.

I had stopped writing here, trying to find the right words to end this chapter. I wanted to inspire and help anyone facing rejection at work. No words came after the paragraph before this one. Then, tonight, I heard President Barack Obama accept the John F. Kennedy Profile In Courage Award. Obama didn't know it, but he helped me, and through me, hopefully he can help you too. He spoke of the courage to stand up to hate and dogma. He urged us to look at our own fears and embrace the courage to make changes or find "principled compromise."

So, I'm asking you to pay attention and speak up if you're facing pronatalistic rejection at work. Progress, as

President Obama said, is "fragile." Step by step we must have the courage to enlighten our colleagues and challenge unfair treatment or expectations at work. We have the capacity to make a difference. It's through us that rejection at work may become a thing of the past.

Chapter 6
Military Stories

*"I am concerned for the security of our great Nation;
not so much because of any threat from without, but
because of the insidious forces working from within."*
—Douglas MacArthur

There's a private war that military personnel face in
the army, navy, air force, marines, and coast guard. Few
know anything about it. It's not the old "Don't ask, don't
tell" bias against gays. It's not the jeers facing returning
service members, as it was in the days of Vietnam. It's a
different kind of clandestine challenge facing a subculture
most people don't recognize. It places nobody in harm's
way. However, the gradual and cumulative psychological
effect can be upsetting and frightening, leading to feelings
of rejection. The subculture is the childfree in the
American military.

Since the military places a huge premium on the
virtues of honor, duty, and loyalty, those who have the
nerve to openly admit they never want to have or raise
kids are looked down upon with distain. They're deemed
to be selfish. They don't fit into the approved
psychological/social matrix of military service. They're not
regarded as honorable. They're considered an
embarrassment to what the military is supposed to
represent: good people who love their country, are ready
to die to protect us, and embrace the traditions of raising
children in America. Although the childfree fit all those
qualifications other than the embrace of raising children,
they're not given the same recognition or perks that are

accorded to serving parents. From what I've heard and researched, they may receive unfair and unequal treatment.

Since the time humans belonged to tribes, recognition and acceptance have been welcomed feelings. They still are, aren't they? Acceptance makes us feel appreciated and part of the group or community we value. When people don't feel accepted in families, at work, or with friends, we often leave those groups. But you can't just walk out of the military!

My awakening to this discrimination came unexpectedly. One of the childfree people who regularly posted on one of my Facebook sites suggested that her military experience of admitting she didn't want children was shocking. She said, "If you think there's prejudices out there against people who don't want to have children, visit any military base and see how the childfree are shunned, disrespected, and not equal to parents serving."

When I asked others to share stories about pronatalism in the military, I received a tsunami of troubling personal experiences. I knew I was onto something that's not openly discussed. Indeed, these revelations were almost always accompanied by a fervent request that I not reveal the commenters' real names, military status, or where they were serving. Apparently, that's how much fear is associated with sharing childfree-by-choice truths in the military.

Because everyone faces the same dangers in their commitment to protect our county, you would think that everyone would receive equal support and acceptance in training, housing, and deployment. Apparently, that's not the way it is. (The exception is training. It's the same for everyone.) However, housing and deployments are not equal. Social ostracization, shunning, and belittlement face anyone who dares to admit they never want to have kids. Worse yet, there's nothing the childfree can do.

Here's where I must admit I know nothing about being in the military. I never had a single friend who was drafted in the past, or enlisted in the present. Although my beloved stepfather served in the Battle of the Bulge, I never thought to question him about pronatalism in the military. Although my best friend Jane's father was a lifetime military man, it never came up in conversation. Both have since died.

This military pronatalism revelation happened in 2017. So, for me, anything about the military is newfound territory. My eyes are getting wider with every account, every share, and every heartfelt experience I've been privileged to become aware of. You might be as shocked as I was after reading this chapter.

Here are a few experiences from our honored military personnel, both active and retired. Some came to me through emails, phone interviews, or articles. A few interviews later in this chapter were conducted via Skype. Every single person, except one who's now retired, begged me not to use his or her real name. I've changed the names to protect their privacy, as many are still serving. The requests for anonymity reveal so much. Parents never say "Don't use my name" when touting their positive stories about raising children in the military. Non-parents tend to be more careful. Fear of rejection permeates their interactions in the military. Rejection may define the childfree as "others" outside of accepted military norms.

Erin: "My husband and I are enlisted in the army.

Military housing, including both overseas housing and in the U.S., is always better for families with children living on any base. Several times, if I complained because we had to take housing off the base, people suggested I get pregnant because I could get a nicer, bigger house in a better location if I had a kid. If I had more than one, it was even better!"

I shook my head in disbelief after reading that statement. Can you imagine anyone choosing to parent for better housing on a military base? Seriously? I didn't know if I wanted to laugh or cry.

Gail: "After serving, it's maddening that a military spouse with children gets priority over me, a disabled veteran, for employment, medical care, and services. My sixteen years of service doesn't seem to matter, nor does my education, language training, experiences, or disability. However, had I married some guy and had a few kids, I'd be at the top of the list for many services or jobs. This is just ridiculous and makes me feel utterly frustrated! I can't do a thing about it, either."

Gail dedicated sixteen years of her life to military service. What was the return? When I asked her if her unequal treatment made her feel she'd made a bad choice to serve, her response was fast: "HELL NO!"

Helen: "I was excitedly waiting to go home for Thanksgiving after a long deployment in a very unpleasant, stressful war zone in the Middle East. The date was set and travel arranged. However, that changed when my superior explained they needed one nurse to stay. Of the three navy nurses (all women) eligible for extensions there, I was the only one without a child. I had to stay because the other two nurses were mothers with children to care for."

Helen was supposed to go home. The mothers were allowed to go while she was kept back. If their children had been ill, I don't think she would have been as upset. Childfree people aren't heartless. However, there was no other reason given than that they had children to care for.

Meagan: "As a woman living on a military base, it's almost impossible to find like-minded or accepting people. Most of the women are either pregnant, trying to get pregnant, upset they weren't pregnant, or aghast if anyone didn't think being a mother was a part of your destiny. I never felt I could tell my truth. Once, someone even suggested I'm a lesbian when I had a brief feeling of courage and confided that I didn't want to have kids. I never said it again. I never felt close to any mother on the base. I longed for my friends at home who supported my choice. I missed the quiet times we shared a glass of wine talking about things other than potty training or what position makes it easier for the sperm to meet the egg!"

I heard about the need for quality military friendships many times. It shows how the childfree hunger to be with like-minded people while serving. There's so much to deal with, and so few genuine friendships to share when people are far from their own families and friends.

Fran: "As a single woman living on the base, many men tried to start something on the side because they were tired of having to deal with kids, family, and commitment. Their wives hated me with contempt, thinking I was trying to lure their husbands away from them. Husbands confided they were told not to speak to me. I think it's kind of silly. After all, I could have ten kids and still want to play on the side!"

Reading this, from a divorced woman, blew me away. I wondered how many women who had kids were hit on? Are childfree women seen as being more promiscuous?

Lauren: "We were invited to a couple of family events. I went because I had to. My husband is the 4th-highest rank in his office. I have to set an 'example' for the lower ranks. I must show I'm supportive and interested in families living there even though I really don't give a damn. I usually sit and listen to all the complaints many have about their endless responsibilities as a mother or their difficulties in pregnancies. It's a good confirmation of the decision I made! The military is a land of breeders!"

I don't like the word "breeders," but I understand why childfree service members might use it. It's rare to hear as negative a word about those who have children. Childfree anger is pent up! Although I did chuckle at Lauren's idea that listening to the complaints of parents was an affirmation of her choice to remain childfree. The truth about raising children might be effective birth control! At least it reminds those who don't want children to take those birth control pills, have an IUD inserted, or research sterilization and vasectomies!

Childfree-by-choice couples serving in the military get the most pressure to procreate. They're constantly asked when they will settle down and have kids. If a wife is on base and her husband is deployed, they'll both be asked how she copes with loneliness without kids to care for. One woman who wrote to me answered that question with, "Well, I take Tai Chi classes, read, get massages, play the guitar, sometimes travel, take online courses, lots of bubble baths, go to the movies, eat out, have my nails done, go to the gym, volunteer, and garden." The reaction was wide-open mouths, as if they wanted to say something but couldn't find the words. One replied to her with contempt: "As if that could take the place of caring for kids? How selfish can you be? You're proud to say that?"

If the husband is serving, married, and has no children, other men who are parents will badger him. One man wrote that he was constantly asked, "When are you going to join our ranks? Are you shooting blanks? Isn't it time when you go home on leave to get to work and give your wife a baby?" He didn't have the nerve to tell them he never wanted to have kids! He didn't think he would be given the same respect as the fathers in his unit. He also couldn't stand the thought of the ribbing he would get. And something else niggled his brain. Would he be protected in harm's way as much as a father who was more revered? It was a troubling thought. (See more about childfree men outside of the service in Chapter 8.)

After reading all the emails that were sent to me, my interest was piqued. I decided to dig deeper. Written words aren't as revealing as conversations, because in conversation I can ask questions. It was astonishing how much more I learned. I placed a call-out on my childfree sites, and many people welcomed me into in-depth conversations. We made phone and Skype dates. Again, all except one retired man and his wife asked that I not use their real names!

The first person I interviewed by phone was a twelve-year commissioned second lieutenant nurse serving in the air force. She took ROTC in college and chose the military as her career. She decided to remain childfree and shared, "I really never liked little kids! Even when I played with my Barbie dolls, they were working Barbies. None wanted kids. I wanted to drive a pink Corvette too! I wanted my own life and not the endless responsibilities of parenting."

I laughed with her, then started to question her, and she interrupted me with, "I must tell you this. My views don't reflect the military or Department of Defense. They're my own personal opinions!"

That startled me. She admitted she was indoctrinated by the military to say this. She knew her revelations didn't reflect what was expected of military women. She felt she had to make me aware that her words were her own, even though she was assured I wouldn't use her real name!

When she entered the military, she claimed, there were times she considered becoming a parent. "It usually happened when my husband, who's a pilot and also enlisted on the same base, was deployed. I wondered if these thoughts occurred because of the expectation forced on us about having kids if you're married. Marcia, the majority of wives on base either have kids or plan to. The women who have kids would start on me, saying I wouldn't be as alone! I really never felt 'alone,' but after thinking more about it, I decided being a parent and remaining in the service wouldn't be good! I would always have to worry about being deployed. My freedom would be severely tested, not to mention when I left the service. It's a forever commitment!"

I asked her if she ever told people she served with that she never wanted to have or raise kids.

"No ma'am!" (I flinched at the word "ma'am." I used to think of "ma'am" as an address for an aging person... which I was! However, I learned it's what military people are expected to say. It's also very Southern.) She continued: "However, among other health care military professionals, I feel a bit more accepted. They seem to understand more than those who live on base out of the medical field. If I would tell those other people, I would get an arched eyebrow or a side-eyed view with a shrug and a sigh, as if I'm nuts! So, I keep it to myself."

When I asked if there were any military experiences she wanted to vent about, it poured from her like lava from a volcano.

"There's so much! First of all, I hate that I must work holidays. Parents get time off to be with their kids. Don't we have people we want to be with? I try to be more understanding, but honestly, I get pissed! We're supposed to be in the same job. We signed the same dotted line! The military didn't issue people kids. They choose to have them. Then, there are the mandatory fun days."

I interrupted her. "The what?"

Her laughter was infectious as she explained: "We're expected to go to family fun days like picnics." (She emphasized *"family FUN days,"* rather sarcastically.) "They're always on a Saturday, which, by the way, is my day off! If I would dare complain, I'd get, 'Well, what do you do with *all* that free time you have, anyhow?'" (Her voice took on a sneer with the word "all.") She continued, "It's beyond parents and higher-up personnel to see what I do with my free time. Even if I told them what I love doing, it would pale in comparison to raising kids. I see value in meditating, reading a book, taking a walk, listening to my favorite music. I don't even go there trying to explain."

"Do you go to those events?" I asked.

She continued: "Yes ma'am. Reluctantly I show up. Guess what? Their kids seem to gravitate to me. Who knows why? Maybe because I'm fun! Maybe because their own parents want some space away from the usual grind of raising them, and ask them to go play! A few mothers, who know I don't want kids, don't like that and take their kids away from me as if I'm a psycho nut. They probably think their kids aren't safe with me because I don't want my own."

That answer resonated within me. I remembered how I lost my job as a teacher after talking about my childfree lifestyle on *60 Minutes* in 1974. I lost my job because of the perception that since I didn't want kids, I probably hated them.

Hearing about the anger she feels as a childfree person, I asked if there was anyone on base she could feel comfortable talking to, such as a psychologist.

"No ma'am! There's supposed to be doctor/client privacy. I doubt it. Some therapists may feel you're not emotionally okay to serve if you don't want kids. If the one you're talking to feels that way, it could have bad effects. If I was physically sick, it's more acceptable than any kind of emotional challenge such as harassment over not wanting kids. Honestly, I never had that need for a therapist anyhow. I'm pretty secure in my choices."

I asked how her childfree choice affected her friendships on and off base.

"Most of the people my age have kids. Sometimes, many kids, two, three, or even four! Friendships are hard to keep because we have nothing in common. It may sound like a cliché, but my husband is my best friend."

I continued, "How do you respond if they ask questions that seem to place you on the defensive as a military person?"

"Oh. The same way I do with anyone on base or at home," she snickered. "I use a lot of humor to deflect their ignorance! I'm pretty blunt, so I try and deflect that way. I may say, 'Kids? I'm the kind that wants to hand them back, not take them home with me!' I try not to escalate any more questions and move away as fast as I can."

Finally, I wanted to know if there was anything positive about being childfree in the military.

She laughed. "Yes! Of course, ma'am. I can pursue my dream of attaining a flight nurse level when I can travel more. I come home to a quiet house. I have more flexibility with what I can do, other than the mandatory 'fun' experiences. I don't have to worry about saving money for the constant wants or needs of kids. But, that's true anywhere!"

I loved speaking with this active-duty air force nurse. It broadened my awareness of inequities in the U.S. military.

Another navy nurse told me this new piece of information:

"Medical care, or lack of as many benefits for me as for a non-parent, upsets me! Mothers get full pregnancy and birthing attention from top-rated doctors. After the birth, this attention and care continues. However, when I had to see a dentist, I had to go to an inferior trained professional, probably a reject from civilian life, who caused me bone damage! If I needed any other medical help, I had to get a referral to the better doctors. It's totally unfair and biased care against singles or marrieds without kids."

My next phone interview was with a childfree couple serving in the army. I started by welcoming them and thanking them for taking the time to help us see the "light" of childfree couples serving in the military.

"Thank you, and you're welcome," she said. "This is hard for us, because there aren't many childfree military couples serving, so it's awkward to openly speak."

I asked the wife if she was looking forward to the opportunity to let it all hang out.

"Very much so! Being childfree in the military is something new and not understood. Also, being in my twenties, if I dared to say anything I would hear I was young and would change my mind."

I asked what specific issues bothered or annoyed them.

"Everywhere you go on post from the Post Exchange (that's our shopping center) to the army community center, you see babies everywhere. A lot of the women on base have two babies on their hips and one in their stroller."

Probing further, I asked, "How does that make you feel?"

"We both feel like the oddball!

Her husband chimed in: "When there's those 'must-attend' family events for your unit, you're the only couple sitting there without kids."

Then he really opened up.

"Even though I have three children from a previous marriage, I never see them. Their mother keeps them away from us. I finally understand the true meaning of being childfree by choice! I'm not a parent or looked upon as one anymore. My kids have nothing to do with me, and probably never will, if their mom keeps poisoning them with lies."

His wife continued: "When I came back from serving in Iraq, I was diagnosed with blocked fallopian tubes.

Truth is, I wasn't always open to being childfree by choice! I was sucked into the myth of babies. With kids everywhere, it was inviting to be seen as one of the revered women on base as a mom. It was very devastating to learn I couldn't have kids. Then, two years later, one tube opened and I surprisingly became pregnant! However, I miscarried. We tried IVF when we were stationed in Japan. We got sick and tired of doing that! I began to wonder if I was doing this to fit in or really wanted to have children. It's also weird because I think I only wanted them, in the beginning, to fit in and because I was told I *couldn't* have them. Before being diagnosed as infertile, I really didn't give kids any thought. I went to the doctor because my husband wanted them at first, being kept from his three kids."

Her husband interrupted: "Now, I totally support our choice to remain childfree by choice!"

She continued: "I'm constantly asked in my unit why I didn't have kids or when am I going to have kids. If I told them the truth, I would get 'Adopt!' Or, 'Try IVF again!' Personally, I feel many military wives keep having kids so they can get additional money from the military and keep their husbands. It sickens me. I've watched people get married and three months later, they're pregnant."

Her husband added, "I see the men slapping that newlywed husband on the back with a 'WAY TO GO' macho salute! However, later, you hear those same men who gave the macho salute complaining about their wives not being interested in sex because they're exhausted from taking care of their kids!"

I laughed, saying it's all part of the myth of being in the accepted parenting tribe no matter what the negatives may be.

Knowing this was an emotional issue for her, I asked the wife if there was anyone she could talk to while serving.

"I never had any support group for being childfree. Your Facebook page was the first I ever came upon about being childfree. I was so relieved to find other people like me. However, no posts were from military people. As I said, I wasn't always childfree by choice, but I try and do what makes me happy. I was the best soldier in my field because I had time to focus on my job."

Her husband continued: "My male co-workers eventually started telling me they envy me and my wife because I could do whatever I wanted with our money and time. When they got off long shifts, they had to deal with their wives and kids! I went home to a wife handing me a margarita and dinner waiting. Many times, I would do the same for her!"

She finished the interview with: "At first, it was difficult to be childfree in the army. Toward the end of our service, our confidence in our choice started setting in. We changed from feeling unsure to feeling lucky. Now, we're retired and have time to travel once a month, go out for dinners, and enjoy our life."

I thanked this couple for their candid and revealing story. Although a lot of what she said mirrored what happens in civilian life, the difference is that in civilian life there are more opportunities to find childfree people to talk with. I smiled to myself at the thought that my Facebook site had been a help to her.

The last person I interviewed was Sharon, a young woman about to join the air force. I thought it would be interesting to see what preconceived ideas a younger woman might have about serving while childfree by choice before she went through basic training.

When she appeared on my computer screen via Skype, I was taken aback. She was stunningly adorable! Her hair was a bright blue-green color and cut at an angle over one side of her face. Her skin was porcelain with no sign of blemish or wrinkle. What did I expect? She was eighteen. I reminded myself to ask her if she thought the military would allow that hair color.

She told me she would be going to basic training a few months later. Her father had been in the army, but she wasn't joining to continue the tradition. She wanted the health care benefits, education, and secure future that the military promised. When I asked what she aspired to, she shouted without hesitation: "Four-star general!"

I loved her spunk and lofty aspirations. She knew there were two women currently serving with that title. I asked her if they were childfree. "Um... no, I believe they have kids." Then, as an afterthought, she said, "I can't imagine how they could do that and get to that rank!"

That's when I asked her when she knew she wanted to remain childfree.

"I believe I was very young. I never liked playing with dolls. Babies, like my brother, annoyed me if I heard them crying. Although I was raised in a strictly Catholic environment and went to a Catholic school, I started doubting that kids would be a part of my life! We were taught they should be! In junior high I asked my mom if I had to have kids. She, said, 'No. You don't have to have kids!'"

Continuing with this train of thought, I asked if she's

shared her point of view with others, and if so, how she's been received.

"I get the usual, 'You'll change your mind, you're too young to know yet.'"

She rolled her eyes as she continued. "I'm too young to know *that*, but not too young to know I want to join the air force?" We both snickered.

"Will you tell others in basic training if it comes up?" I asked.

"Of course! No point in lying" she answered, staring at me with her big, beautiful, dark eyes.

"Do you think your choice will be accepted?" I asked, thinking about the other military responses I'd heard, and wondering if she knew what she was in for.

"I hope so, but if they don't accept me, it won't bother me. I'll do my job to the best of my ability whether or not I'm respected for my personal choice. If they want kids... great! That doesn't affect me."

I knew from our earlier conversation that she was trying to get sterilized. It was a losing battle. One doctor after another told her she was too young. I also knew from my interviews that pronatalism is blatant in the military, and she would have to face the consequences of being a single childfree woman in her military career.

I was between a rock and a hard place. Her face exuded the joy of her commitment. Her excitement was palpable. I didn't want to be a harbinger of unpleasant possibilities.

I took a deep breath and asked, "Do you think there could be any discrimination in, let's say, housing on base? Or extra duties if you have no kids?"

"Discrimination? Uh... no! We all get BAH [Basic Allowance for Housing] based on rank." Then, as if thinking more, she asked, "Why? Is there?"

Not wanting to be the one to let her down, I switched to another question and asked what she would do if she was given extra duties because she was childfree and others were parents.

"I would go to my commanding officer and complain!" she triumphantly shouted.

"And," I continued, "if your commanding officer didn't care, or felt you were whining, what would you do?"

She paused, mulling this over. Her bravado waned. "Well, I would suck it up and not do anything more! I'm a pretty tough woman!" She paused, as if thinking to herself, and finally asked, wide-eyed and a bit concerned, "Hey! Are you saying I'm going to experience these things?"

I didn't have the heart to burst her bubble.

I carefully tiptoed around the issue, saying, "Everyone faces his or her own experiences. Maybe you should keep a journal and come back to me after serving a bit to see what your actual experiences as a committed childfree woman are in the military.

She eagerly responded, "Wow! Great idea!"

Before our Skype experience ended I had one more question: "Sharon, do you plan on keeping your wild blue-green iridescent hair?"

"Of course not," she said, laughing! "I know I have to go back to my usual acceptable color."

I wondered to myself about her desire to be sterilized and never have kids in the air force. The hair might be the least of her awakenings in the service. I hope her days are fulfilling and she never has the negative experiences I heard about from others who serve in the military.

Two years after I first interviewed Sharon, I saw her

reappear on Facebook. I asked her how she was. She said she was getting married! I wished her well and kept watching for her posts. There were lovely photos of her and her husband. Then she shared that she was training for another profession. She admitted she "left the military." I'm hoping it wasn't from bitter disillusionment.

Childfree-by-choice people living on a military base feel as if they're swimming against the current in a sea of parents and children. They're not given the same status as parents. They're expected to do more than parents. They're constantly asked when they will settle down. Friends are difficult to make because there's a lack of common experience to share.

So what can childfree people do to deal with the rejection and the expectations? That depends. Those who have a long time left to serve, and those who have thinner skins against prejudice, may do best to play the game to win. If directly asked why there are no children, you can just smile and stare off with a sigh. Maybe look a little wistful? They'll never know you're secretly thinking, *Because I love being childfree!* Or, as the air force nurse I interviewed suggested, deflect with humor.

For others who are proud of their lifestyle choice and feel it's worth sharing, go for it. Tell your truths with the same conviction with which you share other choices. If things get too confrontational and you feel it's useless to continue, ask people if they are happy as parents. Most will say they are. You can end by saying, "That's great! That's exactly how I feel about not wanting to have them."

As for housing, there's not much you can do. Look forward to when you can rise in rank or leave the service and find your sweet nest filled with peace and comfort, not the steady demands of parenting.

If you're forced to go to family events on base, daydream about the joys of not having to deal with that kind of thing once you're out of the military. As one of my interviewees shared, "It's really a good lesson about what you're *not* going to miss!"

If you hunger for like-minded friendships, be bold! Seek out people on the base without kids. Tell them you're thinking about not having children. Are they? If they say, "Of course I want kids!" keep going.

If you're reading this book and are in the military, it must be refreshing to find out you're not alone in feeling like an "other" as a childfree person. We can only hope that the more you speak up with pride and conviction, the sooner the tide of ignorance, inequality, and pronatalism will end.

In the quote at the start of this chapter, Douglas MacArthur, a five-star American general in World War II, questioned whether our nation was "secure." He alluded to insidious forces working from within, not from without, that could undermine that security. After writing this chapter, I asked myself if our service members who are willing to die for our country yet aren't accepted or respected for their childfree choice feel secure themselves. How does that lack of acceptance affect them as they fight for the safety of our nation? How does it affect them to have few close friendships and be denied equal housing? The military is one institution where everyone should feel equal and protected. Are they?

To all the childfree-by-choice service members: we acknowledge what you face. Stay proud. Ask for equality, as the LGBTQ community has done. Speak your mind if you're presented with prejudice that affects your time in the service.

To all those who have served, are now serving, or will serve, no matter what your lifestyle choices are, we thank you.

Chapter 7
The NotMom Summit

"In a deeply tribal sense, we love our monsters, and I think that is the key to it right there. It is monsters; it is learning about them: it is both thrill and safety. You can think of them without being desperately afraid because they are not going to come into your living room and eat you. That is 'Jaws.'"
—Peter Benchley

Most childfree people yearn to be with like-minded people. The empathy we receive from those who understand how we feel is treasured. The shared stories of rejection by friends, family, co-workers, and even strangers are welcomed. We don't like to hear about the pain of rejection from others, but it validates our own. We're not alone.

That's why I chose to accept the invitation to attend the second NotMom Summit in Cleveland, Ohio, in October of 2017. I wanted to reach more people, validate this lifestyle, and feel the euphoria that comes from helping people heart to heart. I wanted to learn more, to see what I could do to make this lifestyle even more viable.

I was asked to present the first keynote speech at this summit. I can say without hesitation that it was a redefining and enlightening moment of my life.

It's important to note that this gathering was not specifically for the childfree-by-choice. The childless were also warmly welcomed. There's quite a difference between choosing never to have or raise a child and infertility. The infertile face a biological stab in the heart. It's a rude awakening to learn that you can't participate in the common destiny of raising a family. The word "childless" is accompanied by the tsk-tsk-tsking of society at all they'll miss. They face pity. Many think of themselves as failures. Talk about a challenge as the first proudly childfree keynote speaker! I knew there were many childless listening to me who were aching to have children.

There was yet another group at the summit who, though they always craved raising children, knew they carried the genes for terrible mental or physical challenges in their potential offspring. Bravely and consciously taking responsibility, they didn't want to bring life into this world burdened with those challenges.

Finally, there were women who had lost a fetus prior to birth and couldn't conceive again. I knew many of them were there to work through their grief, accept that their bodies were not going to bear a child for whatever reason, and come to understand their lot as freedom, not lack.

I carefully planned my speech in the knowledge that all those women would be listening. The childfree by choice were easier to reach than those who were childless. I lived that first lifestyle. I spoke about that lifestyle. I wrote about that lifestyle. I was interviewed many times on TV, in newspapers, and on radio about that lifestyle. Having never faced infertility or had to choose against procreation out of respect for danger to a child, I was fearful I might come on too strong and hurt those feeling rejected by their bodies. Would I *not* do justice to those who never wanted children by tiptoeing around issues that could offend the childless? It took me weeks of writing and rewriting. I went to sleep thinking about this speech. I woke up thinking about the lives I might reach. I drove my husband Jim crazy revising the PowerPoint that accompanied my speech. (Jim is a computer guru who has a computer business. Yes, I know! I'm lucky for that and many other reasons.)

I wasn't truly aware of what this conference meant to those who were trying to move from acceptance of their childlessness to childfree by choice. Could I be the catalyst giving them power to change their goals in life? Were worthy goals even necessary in the planning of personal lives? Could it be okay to simply enjoy life without defining an altruistic path?

It was only after my speech that I had an aha moment. Even with all my past speaking engagements and Internet presence, I wasn't savvy about the deeply troubling feelings the childless experience. My body never betrayed me. I never even tried to have a child! I didn't have mental or physical issues other than the usual heart disease or cancer in my family's lineage.

I walked up to that podium, heart pounding in my chest, and did my best. It felt good. I had practiced that speech to perfection in front of a mirror. I knew it was connecting by the occasional loud applause and laughter, and the eyes glued to my PowerPoint presentation and me. I included photos of myself as a child with my favorite doll, showing how I was programmed to feel that being a "mommy" was in my future. I included the pronatalistic ads from Campbell's Soup that imprint us with "It's not soup 'til mother makes it!" I shared what happened to me after my *60 Minutes* TV interview, which led to death threats, picketing when I spoke, and the loss of my teaching job. I ended with an impassioned request that everyone keep their minds and hearts open to the joys of a childfree lifestyle. I warned of the continued societal brainwashing that makes childfree people feel "less than" instead of perfect just the way they are.

After my speech was over, there was raucous applause and a standing ovation. I felt tears brimming, and knew I'd had a positive impact. As my speech concluded that part of the day's program, women rushed up to hug me. Many told me how much they appreciated my being there.

I was riding on cloud nine until the next morning. A breakfast panel discussion was planned featuring awesome women from around the world. They would share their international perspectives on being childfree. This experience led to the twelfth chapter in this book: "Facing Worldwide Rejection." One woman on that panel was Jodi Day, a well-known and revered British childless-by-fate author/speaker/motivator. Meeting her that day and hearing her speak helped me to understand many things I'd never known about being childless.

However, when I walked into the presentation area, which had been filled with chatting, animated women the day before, I felt a pang of apprehension. There were fewer attendees than yesterday! Many of the tables had several empty seats! What happened? Could people have overslept after drinking too many cosmos the night before? Maybe some people hadn't purchased the two full days of lectures and break-out sessions? There was an almost somber mood. It was palpable. Maybe they needed some coffee? Or was it something I didn't want to think about? Could I have had something to do with this smaller turnout? My insecurity startled me, because I'm usually very positive and secure about myself.

After getting my cup of coffee and a wonderful buffet

breakfast, I took a seat at one of the tables in front of the podium. In a few minutes, I was more focused on what this distinguished panel was sharing than on what might have caused the diminished attendance.

When the panel discussion ended, these women got another standing ovation. Then they asked for questions and comments. The usual questions were heard: Did you have problems with your family? If you were infertile, how did you come to terms with being unable to conceive? How can we find other people who understand our feelings? Internationally, is getting a tubal ligation easy or difficult? But the last commenter reverberated with me for a long time. Her remarks still linger as a lesson to me, and now, hopefully, for you.

Someone passed the mic to a young woman in the audience. She was adorable, well-groomed and beautifully dressed. Her hair was pulled back off her oval face. With a hint of lip gloss glittering as she spoke, she hesitantly started her question while still seated. A few people asked her to rise and speak more directly into the mike. Her voice was very soft. (She didn't appear to be a person who frequently raised her hand.) With a quivering voice, she said, "I'm sad to observe many of the childfree-by-fate women, like myself, not returning today. I think it's because of hearing from Marcia Drut-Davis yesterday!"

My head spun around.

She continued: "A few of my childless friends told me last night they couldn't take her happiness as a childfree-by-choice woman. Why did they feel disappointed? I loved hearing from her! She gave me hope. She gave me insights into why I may have felt unworthy as a woman due to pronatalism."

Jodi Day took the microphone. In her beautifully composed British accent, she said, "Marcia's speech was an awesome, inspiring message about the childfree lifestyle."

I looked at her gratefully, trying to hold back the tears. I would never want anyone to feel threatened by my message.

Jodi smiled directly at me and then, turning to the young woman who had asked the question, she said, "However, many aren't ready to hear about her excitement and joy. They haven't gone through what I call the gray area from grief over rejection by their bodies to acceptance that they'll never have or raise a child. It's too threatening. They're not ready for possible happiness. They still need to grieve!"

Many heads nodded, showing acknowledgment and understanding.

Jodi continued: "The five stages of grief were originally theorized by Elisabeth Kübler-Ross, and include denial, anger, bargaining, depression, and acceptance. I'm guessing that those who left had not experienced one or more of those stages. Acceptance wasn't felt."

The young woman said, "Thank you. It's sad they'll miss your keynote tonight!" and sat down.

Although I was somewhat appeased, I still felt a stab of pain and rejection at the thought that I had caused unhappiness when I only wanted to inspire, support, and illuminate the potential in the childfree lifestyle.

As that session ended, I slowly walked out of the large meeting room. Before I exited, a woman stopped me, pulled me aside, and said, "You have no idea what you've just done for my life!" I hugged her and we walked out together. She grabbed my sleeve and ushered me farther away from the crowd and said, "I have to tell you something." She started to cry. She couldn't even talk! I held her close and sat down on the floor with her until her crying stopped. She trembled in my arms.

Soon she regained her composure.

After we stood up together I noticed she was the same height as me. Her brown hair cascaded straight around her pretty face. Her eyes were red from crying. Her tears had smudged mascara on her cheeks.

"I've suffered from infertility for too long. I read your book. It helped. But hearing you today, I know now I'm at acceptance! How do I thank you?"

Tears came back to both of us. "You just did," I softly whispered as we hugged again.

When I got home, another fan of mine posted a photo of us together at that summit and wrote on my Facebook support site: "They say when you meet your hero, you'll be disappointed. I wasn't!" I love you, Blair.

I can't find the words on this keyboard to tell you how it feels to touch another person the way I've been blessed to do.

I went back to my room and cried. Some of the tears were unhappy. I felt rejected by some of the people I tried to reach. And though it truly was unintentional, they felt rejected by me. Whatever I did wasn't enough. This affected how I went on to treat the many childless people I meet who admit they're still trying to accept being unable to conceive. It's a new pocket of the childfree lifestyle I don't think I was prepared for. Now, with the benefit of their reactions and the help of Jodi Day, I am.

Other tears came from feeling grateful, overwhelmed,

and humbled. I wondered if Ellen Peck ever knew how her eye-opening book *The Baby Trap* affected my life. Did I tell her enough? Did she ever go home and cry, as I'd done, over the reactions of those she's reached? We became friends and worked together on the first National Convention of Non-Parents in 1974, but I can't remember shedding a tear in front of her. I hope I did at least once!

This understanding of the pain and rejection that the childfree and childless go through recently touched me again via my closed page on Facebook. Most of the people in this group are childfree by choice. Many, however, are childless and looking for acceptance, yearning to hear from those who love their childfree lifestyle. They get tired of well-meaning people telling them of yet another IVF treatment or surrogacy or adoption option. They may belong to Internet support groups for the childless and don't want to hear more crying, whining, or complaining. They're done! Their quest for that baby is over!

Both groups come to my site to share articles, ask questions, and sometimes vent. Some are very, very angry. Their personal pain over rejection morphs into words I find personally offensive. Words such as "mombies" and "moos" (meaning mothers who act sanctimonious about birth) bother me. There's also "devil's spawn" and "crotch droppings" (meaning children) and "breeders," which is self-explanatory.

Childfree people who feel rejection may have a need to vent using such distasteful phrases. They're in a safe place where they know others will support their posts. Many followers of my site give them "likes," "loves" and "hahas." But childless people don't feel comfortable using those words. They once wanted to be the very women who are being called "moos."

From time to time, a childfree person announces they're finally getting a tubal ligation or vasectomy. That gets tons of "woot-woots" and "way to gos" from followers. There's a new push to throw parties to celebrate such final birth control choices, a counterpoint to the baby showers that many people feel obligated to attend and truly don't enjoy. They say the gifts at such parties are very funny: wine for casual evenings without worry about getting drunk, tickets to movies, dinner reservations, travel brochures, best-selling books to read in peace, and other creative ways to share their pleasure in the childfree lifestyle.

However, for the few child*less* who come to my site searching for acceptance as child*free*, it may hurt. Read this and see what my administrators and I have faced:

"Marcia, I'm going off your site. I can't take the joy and accolades in announcing someone's having a tubal or being 'spayed' like their cat. For me, who can't have children, it's too hurtful. I also can't take the ugly words some use aimed at parents. Why do people do that? I still love you but have to leave."

I sympathized with this woman. Being a classic Libra, I wanted everyone coming to my site to feel honored and helped. Having been to the NotMom Summit, my consciousness was raised to understand the pain that the childless face. I felt proud that any childless person would come to my childfree site. I also knew that childless and childfree mean different things to different people. My sites are known to be supportive of those who never want to have children. Some of the venting that people feel free to share there could possibly hurt those who haven't changed their mindset from childless to childfree. I knew their goal was acceptance, not more personal rejection as a failure. I decided to take a poll on our site. I asked almost two thousand followers whether they approved of the rather crude, distasteful words mentioned before. The results were overwhelmingly in favor of maintaining that option on our closed site. They appreciated the chance to vent in a safe place. Although I really don't like the disparaging words, it's not my opinion that counts. It's what the majority clearly needed.

I would like to offer the childless the understanding that we, the childfree by choice, can stand as a beacon of hope to childlessness. We, who live this lifestyle, can offer our truths to help overturn years of social and religious brainwashing and prove that life can be wonderful, exciting, and meaningful without raising a human. We can share the meaning that life offers us in our commitment to each other, to animals, and to this planet. For some of us, it's honoring our commitment to our inner child and doing whatever floats our boats. Not every childfree person follows an altruistic path. We don't have to prove anything to a society that labels us selfish.

Sometimes, being with like-minded people helps us to fight the monsters we may face as a societal "other." An affirming tribe can help us see that our personal choices are perfectly fine.

It's my fervent hope in writing this chapter that you'll make it a goal to change one person's brainwashed view about the childfree lifestyle from negative to positive. Speak with words that teach, not attack. Speak proudly and with the same passion that parents speak with. Speak with compassion about the challenges that childless people must overcome.

Who is that one person you can reach? It may not be your mom, dad, grandparents, siblings, friends, or co-workers. That one person may be you.

Chapter 8
Childfree Men

"The heart of a father is the masterpiece of nature."
—Antoine François Prévost d'Exiles

"Certainly the best works, and of greatest merit for the public, have proceeded from the unmarried or childless men."
—Francis Bacon

I've noticed a growing emphasis in the childfree movement toward the inclusion of more men. Men are coming forward on my Facebook sites, blog, Instagram, and Twitter to voice or vent their concerns over inequality and ask for validation.

When I started noticing more childfree men on social media, I asked, "Childfree men, what's your pet peeve about the childfree lifestyle?" The most common response by far was the difficulty of finding a like-minded life partner. Many women seem to feel that if a man doesn't want kids, he's not marriage material.

The second-most-common response was that men don't feel they can be authentic at work. They fear saying anything about living a childfree life. "It's better if they think I can't have kids," said Alan. One woman put her two cents in with, "My husband won't dare say anything. He gets too much ribbing about not doing 'it' enough!"

That made me chuckle, as if doing "it" has anything to do with having or not having a child. A couple can be sexually active and take precautions against procreating. In fact they can be sterilized, and nobody would or should know that! Then there are couples trying to conceive who have sex as much as they can, only to face infertility.

Alan responded, "Because men with kids are considered to be a 'family man.' They seem to get the promotions. It's as if having kids means you're a better person doing your job. You're viewed as being more complete, more capable, and evolved. It's simply more acceptable. If I told the truth, I could be seen as selfish or hedonistic, not a hard-working man trying to support a family."

Jeff chimed in with, "I feel the same way. There's another issue. At work, if you dare say you don't want kids, you're thought of as not needing as much money as fathers. So, I'm also quiet."

Why is a childfree man seen as less "complete"? Don't all people have a need to make more money? Why is money only important for raising children? How many non-parents have health challenges, or parents in need, or siblings with kids in need, or just the desire to enjoy a well-earned vacation?

Mark added, "If you think you get pressure and I don't because I'm gay, forget about it! At work, I'm constantly bombarded with questions about adopting or surrogacy. It's as if our marriage isn't complete without a child. I fought so hard to marry my partner. Now the pressure to have a child boggles my mind. Our families also keep asking about kids. Getting out of the gay closet seems more acceptable than saying you never want to raise children. I may have escaped one closet, only to dive back into another."

This revelation struck me as profoundly sad. He's won in one war only to be plunged into another. Why is it a war? When can he feel peace? I have no answers. The only peace is found within.

There were more responses that I took to reveal a growing trend toward outspokenness among childfree men:

Don: "Yeah! I get the same bullshit from family. My wife's family actually cornered me and lectured me about having kids. Even though my wife told them neither of us wanted kids long before we met, they're convinced that it's just me and I 'brainwashed' her or something. They've said we're not really a family without kids."

Seth: "I don't want kids. I also don't want an Apple watch, dance lessons, or a pet. Why doesn't anyone pressure me about those things?"

Adam: "One pattern I've noticed is that when I let acquaintances know I'm not interested in having children, they usually default to asking how my wife feels about it, or they tell me it doesn't matter because it's up to my wife! Really? Hell no! What am I? Just a sperm donor without a brain making my own decisions?"

Caleb: "I get the same bullshit I hear women get. 'Why don't you have kids? It'll change when you have your own... you'll see.' Blah, blah, blah. Haven't elected for the vasectomy. Thought about it, but haven't gone that far. Honestly, the idea of working on or around my dick doesn't make me jump for joy. It's worse in small towns. They think you're a failure if you don't marry and breed."

John: "When I told my doc I wanted a vasectomy, he responded with, 'What happens if you meet a woman who wants kids?' WTF! It's me who doesn't want kids. If I meet a woman who does, it's a deal breaker!"

Eric: "Having a vasectomy shows any woman I'm

meeting how much I'm dedicated to not having kids. If they want them, they must pass and find another man."

Sam: "If I tell my truth about not wanting to be a father, I get, 'You should have at least one!' Someone tell me why I should do that when I'm clearly not committed to being a dad. Who would want me taking on that role when I can't stand the idea of the whole fucking lifestyle? If I had 'just one' and hated it, then what?"

David: "I keep my choice to myself. It's none of anyone's business how I live my own life. I have one friend who constantly asks me when I'm having kids. I shrug my shoulders and walk away. Let him think I can't! Sometimes, I really think he's jealous of my free time with none of the endless, ongoing-drama of raising kids that he tells me about day after day."

Tim: "For me, having a vasectomy was the right choice. My wife would have to endure a more involved surgical procedure far worse than what I went through. When I tell my friends I never want kids and had a vasectomy, they look at me wide-eyed. I think some men see procreation as a symbol of masculinity. Yet, once they father a kid, many aren't there to be the daddy kids want. They say their work keeps them too busy. Sure it does."

Jacob: "I have a super-religious family. To them, 'Go forth and multiply' is one's mission in life. I had to promise I would accept children lovingly into my life when I married. Shit no! It was easier to lie than to tell the truth and risk not being able to be married by my wife's priest. I'd probably be excommunicated as a family member. Come to think of it, maybe that wouldn't be all that bad!"

Brad: "Little girls are raised playing house and being a mommy. I played ball with my buddies or video games.

Shooting and annihilating don't equate to parenting. Never once did I think, 'Someday I'll be a father. Yippee.' I did hear my father tell me after I was being a shit, 'Wait! Wait till you're a father. You'll get it then.' I never wanted to get it."

Aden: "All my life I wanted to own a red Corvette. Never once did I see myself bouncing a little kid on my knee. A car isn't the same as a kid, is it? There were times I viewed parenting as what you do after you marry, if you marry at all. Now I don't see it that way. I see my friends who are dads and I can't fathom doing what they do. Those first years of primal screams in the night, sloppy diapers, endless child-centered needs. Nope. Not for me."

Ralph: "Can I be honest? I can't say a pregnant woman is beautiful. Then, after that birth? Sorry, it's not the same. I mean if men love that, fine. Not me. It may sound immature or crass. Their bodies are changed forever. It's real feelings. I never want to see anything coming out of a vagina except my penis."

This last statement got a few comments from women!

Sheila: "I get what you're feeling, Ralph. But, it's also part of the misogynous way some men view women all the time. We have to remain perfect. Guess what? We're far from that and it's fine!"

Rose responded: "He said, 'If men love that, fine. Not me.' He was being honest about a personal feeling."

This seemed to end that confrontation.

Here's a response from Edwin I'm still giggling over. He posted it on one of my "Confessions" pages on Facebook:

"Since this is a 'confessions' page, I have an actual confession. Backstory: my boss at work is a total Mombie*.

She has two kids and thinks being a parent is the most amazing experience in the world (and anyone who hasn't popped out a baby is the scum of the earth). Anyhow, a few weeks ago, I needed to take one day of PTO. I got denied because the 1st quarter is our busiest time of year and we are down two people on our team. Lo and behold, the single mom I work with states that she needs three days off to take her son to Legoland or some shit like that. She gets approved to take off work! WTF?

"Here's where my confession comes in. I knew I had to use the kid angle to get some time off, but I obviously don't have one sitting around the house. I went to my boss and let her know that my wife and I were thinking about trying to have kids, but things weren't 'working' (if you catch my drift). I needed some time off to reset and get things back in balance. My PTO was approved and I was permitted to take three days off, all on the premise that I was basically going to knock boots with my wife to make a baby! Little does she know, I actually just needed to take my dogs to the vet for their annual checkup, so I guess I was technically taking care of my 'kids'?"

*Mombie is slang for a mom who is like a zombie about motherhood and children.

Although I howled with laughter reading Edwin's confession, it saddened me that he had to lie about his reason for wanting time off.

What these childfree men shared is not far from what childfree women feel. Many families accuse women of "brainwashing" a partner into not wanting kids, when both partners truly don't want that lifestyle. It's like families can't accept the fact that a couple doesn't want kids. Someone has to be at fault!

I found the honesty of one man who doesn't want a vasectomy due to fear of having his genitals touched by a doctor... interesting. The procedure is far easier than what a woman must go through to be sterilized.

Pronatalistic pressure affects men just like women!

1. You should have just one! Why? What if you hate being a parent?

2. Once they're your own, you'll love them. Seriously? Then why are there so many horror stories of abuse?

3. Religion produces pressure to procreate, forcing men to lie during Catholic marriage ceremonies.

Some other witty comments from men made me laugh out loud: wanting a red Corvette and not a bouncing baby, not seeing pregnancy as beautiful, not wanting to see anything coming out of a vagina except his penis. (This last was my favorite.)

Here's another insightful reaction to a new trend.

Joshua: "Recently, I couldn't get out of attending a men's baby shower. You just read that right. It was for my bro-in-law. Seems to be the new thing. I stayed as long as I could stomach the nonsense. Smelling baby diapers smeared with foods to see if you know what foods they are and other silly games? If that was me, I would scream, 'Shoot me now!'"

I can feel Joshua's pain. Long ago I stopped going to baby showers unless the mom is directly related to me or a very close friend's daughter. (I never was invited to any man's baby shower.) I prefer sending a gift. It's usually a new nightie for the mom or condoms for the father!

As more men started sharing on my sites, they began to see that it was okay to say how they felt. There were endless responses to the question I posed. The more men saw others commenting, the more reactions I got.

Andrew: "How many fathers don't even live with their kids? Divorce is the norm. I couldn't bear to think if that happened to me. I would have to spend every weekend with the kids and pay my wife child support. Then, if she remarried, I'd have to deal with that man, too. Now, I hear men are getting child support from the mothers of their kids if they have a higher income. They may be forced to remain at home with the kids. In any case, it sucks having a broken family. Nope. Don't need to chance that statistic!"

Jason: "Here's my truth. The woman I screwed got pregnant. We both used contraception. I begged her to consider an abortion. She refused. I'm left with child support. I have nothing to do with the kid. I'm considered to be a cad. If she chose abortion, she wouldn't be as much of a cad as me with the pro-choice movement. Right?"

Terrance: "Isn't anyone concerned with what's happening to our planet? I am. Overpopulation is real. Natural resources are dwindling. At the rate population is growing, we're headed for frightening consequences globally."

Chad: "How many men think about how much it costs to raise one kid? I don't have that kind of money. No thank you. My mom once said, 'Oh, Chad. Kids bring their own good fortune.' Seriously? Even if I partnered with a woman who makes more money than me, I couldn't stand the thought of being a stay-at-home dad. I would go out of my freakin' mind."

More good points from these men: the agony of divorce with children, child support when there's no connection, the consequences of overpopulation, birth control that doesn't work. Hearing these issues raised by so many men was refreshing, as it's usually women expressing these concerns.

Every now and then, more women would chime in:

Jessica: "I've asked my husband if he thinks he's less of a man because our bloodline and his name stopped when he decided not to father a son. He was sure he would allow his brother to have those honors. 'Who gives a shit' was his reply."

Carrie: "Even though my husband had a vasectomy, I still use birth control. Yes! It's that important to us. I've heard of men having vasectomies and fathering a kid. Not taking one chance."

The outpouring of comments from men, and from some women, was like a dam bursting. Once one comment posted, a flood of others followed. It was cathartic for these men to see their feelings and opinions being acknowledged and validated. For some, it may have been the first time. Although many topics are discussed on my support sites, they're rarely addressed by men. Don't get me wrong. Men *do* answer. But the number of responding women exceeds them. My hope is that these forums gave them the push to feel confident in telling their truths.

Now, as I type this, I'm planning another group cruise. This time, one of my guest speakers is a man. When I made that announcement, I swear I could hear the applause affirming his desire to speak. One man wrote to me, "It's about time we heard from a man!" I agree.

Isn't it true that even now, in 2019, the myth that fatherhood is proof of love between partners continues? Although I hate to admit it, I watch the insanely silly TV shows *The Bachelor* and *The Bachelorette*. The primary goal of finding a mate is fetishized in images of fatherhood and motherhood. Every single male participant, bar none, includes kids in his fantasy future. Seriously? Men see this as what women want. Here's the question: Is this what men really want? Or is it just something society has promoted as normal and expected?

Recently, a bachelor on that TV show asked a prospective wife about kids. She responded, "I want fur-kids with four paws." She was rejected! I almost fainted with joy at her honesty.

I opened this chapter with a quote: "The heart of a father is the masterpiece of nature." I was lucky! My father's and stepfather's hearts were their gifts to humankind, and to me. Both were dedicated to helping others. My father was a dedicated teacher. My stepfather was the kindest man his family, friends, and co-workers ever knew. Both taught me what true love and commitment meant. They took time to be with me, laugh, and help me when I faced life's challenges. Both made my life very special.

In my opinion, a masterpiece of nature is how a person helps others, non-sentient beings, and the planet. This isn't always done by procreating or raising children.

That's why I chose the second quote at the start of this chapter: "Certainly the best works, and of greatest merit for the public, have proceeded from the unmarried or childless men."

Here's a partial list of men who I feel were masterpieces of nature by virtue of what they gave to us without procreation: George Washington, Jesus Christ, the Dalai Lama, the Wright brothers, Oliver Wendell Holmes, George Bernard Shaw, Beethoven, Tchaikovsky, Vivaldi,

George Balanchine, Dr. Seuss, Thoreau, Virgil, Spinoza, and the present governor of California, Jerry Brown.

Throughout history, many well-known men have opted not to have or raise kids. Here's another short list of historical men who were never fathers:

James Buchanan, the fifteenth president of the United States. There are rumors he may have been gay. Some say he was asexual. He did have his niece, Harriet Lane, move into the White House as a sort of hostess because there was no first lady. Harriet was an orphan.

T.S. Eliot: Although this famous poet married twice, he had no kids.

Milton Hershey: He founded Hershey's chocolate. He had a bad relationship with his father. We don't know if this caused him and his wife to not have kids, or if they couldn't. The couple did a lot of philanthropic work with children and left the legacies of the Hershey Foundation and Penn State's Milton S. Hershey Medical Center.

Thomas Wolfe: The author of *Look Homeward, Angel* and *You Can't Go Home Again* died at age thirty-eight, having never married or had children.

Edgar Allan Poe: The treasured American writer never had children.

Louis Armstrong: The great trumpet player never had kids.

There are also many unfamous men who give us joy in their dedication to their careers, whether as doctors, educators, artists, musicians, or scientists, or who perform simple acts of love such as volunteering through Meals on Wheels to serve wholesome meals to aging people. Are their hearts any less a masterpiece because they never had or raised children?

Is the heart of a father the "masterpiece" of nature? For some, maybe. They love their role and enjoy being fathers in every aspect of the word. For them, it's their reason for being. Their children are loved and know it. Their children get the benefit of a role model who cares about them. Their partners enjoy shared parenting experiences. Those children are lucky.

However, many men who chose to be fathers don't remotely fit the masterpiece-of-nature description. They're hardly present. They may blame their work, choosing to stay late or go out with other men in their inner circle of co-workers. They may be authoritatively or abusively controlling. They may have no patience. They want the status, the societal acceptance, and the validation, but they don't deliver what's needed from them. Nurturing, patience, commitment, and the skill of listening are unknown to them. They've never had an education in what it means to be a parent, so they can't be blamed. Many have never looked at themselves honestly to ask if they are parent material. Many leave their partners to fend for themselves and their children. Many don't give a damn. Yet they have the esteemed title of "father."

In the 2018-midterm elections, not one of the male candidates was childfree or childless. In fact, Ron DeSantis, a Florida candidate for governor, had a TV ad centered on his being a father! What does that have to do with the office he's running for? The sad fact is that political candidates are seen as more appealing if they have a family with more than one child.

Donald Trump parades his children, from three different women, as people of accomplishment. When

Bernie Sanders ran for the Democratic presidential nomination in 2016, he mentioned his four kids and seven grandkids. What does this have to do with being president of the United States? Yet to judge by all the flyers, postcards, and TV ads that assailed me every day, every single male candidate running for local office touted their status as fathers. Many pamphlets or TV commercials included photos of the candidates with their arms around their children.

Laura Scott, author of *Two Is Enough*, wisely noted that there are many ways to nurture and create rewarding heart connections and love without having or raising children. I go a step further: loving yourself may be the most important heart connection there is. Take care of yourselves though better nutrition, exercise, and regular doctor exams. That includes those prostate exams! Look in the mirror and love yourself with respect and kindness. You're fine just the way you are. Kids won't change that, anyhow.

To your own selves be true. If you don't want children, it's okay! In fact, it's one awesome lifestyle. Don't defend it. Live it with pride.

If you miss nurturing, reach out and see the benefits of helping others. Something amazing happens when you enjoy doing that. There are too many people in need of your masterpiece heart. This doesn't mean you have to help kids. It's perfectly fine not to like them, as long as they're not harmed.

Find rich and rewarding friendships. Strong male friendships radiate and receive reciprocal nurturing. Too many men don't know the joys of childfree male friendships. There's a special bond where you can see friendship in a new light and enjoy like-minded conversation that's not concentrated on children.

You can even be close friends with parents! Once a parent feels safe sharing their challenges as a parent, you'll find a heart connection. Of course, keep your boundaries clear. If child-talk gets too overwhelming, stop it. Change the topic immediately. If you can share an interest in sports, do that. It will take the attention off stories about kids.

If you want to nurture kids without having or raising them, check out the many organizations in dire need of volunteers and mentors: schools, Boys & Girls Clubs, and Big Brothers Big Sisters are a few well-known and respected places to start.

If you have nieces or nephews and you enjoy them, reach out to them. Let yourself be a soft place they can land if they need you. Maybe there are neighbors who need the friendship of a male role model. So many kids are from broken homes, missing their dads.

Finally, be proud of who you are. You have the right to choose whatever lifestyle your magnificent heart desires. Nobody has the right to demean it, condemn it, or force his or her personal choices on you. This is not a dress rehearsal. This is the only life we know. Live it well. Your heart can be a masterpiece without the title of father.

Chapter 9
Facing Rejection Worldwide

"Nothing in all the world is more dangerous than sincere ignorance and conscientious stupidity."
—Martin Luther King Jr.

Being an outspoken childfree woman, author, blogger, Facebook site creator, winner of a lifetime achievement award, and guest speaker for the lifestyle, I've personally faced the realities and heartaches of rejection. Being deemed an "other" can be devastating in any society where having and raising children is the accepted and expected norm.

I was born and raised in the United States, where diversified lifestyles are gaining acceptance. The LGBTQ world is finally gaining more recognition. Non-religious humanist, atheist, and agnostic organizations are gaining membership. However, the childfree lifestyle is still shunned. Many non-parents are estranged from family and friends simply because of their personal choice to not have or raise children. They're considered aberrations, unworthy of heart connections or family ties. It doesn't matter how responsible a life they're living! It doesn't matter if they're happy. Many are challenged.

My experience of rejection in America comes from a personal perspective, and is the result of having gained some notoriety in the lifestyle. However, I have no knowledge about rejection in other countries. How could I? I never was part of any other cultural, societal, or religious indoctrination, aside from what I encountered with my students as an ESL teacher, or as a tourist. Being a tourist doesn't come close to being born and raised abroad.

With more and more people reaching out to me from all over the world, seeking validation or a chance to vent, I started to question whether life in other countries is better, worse, or the same as life in America. That's when I went on a worldwide search for personal reactions to having chosen the childfree lifestyle. Did people internationally face the same kind of rejection that Americans complain about? With each new revelation from abroad, I was awestruck. With each new eye-opening share, I became empowered to reach more people. I kept hearing, "I never have a chance to speak so openly about this in my country!" which spurred me on to find more and more people willing to share their thoughts with me via private message, email, letters, and Skype.

For some, sharing with me was the *first time* they'd felt totally comfortable discussing their childfree issues. What blew me away is how often people needed to share with me more than their rejection as childfree people. It made me think of the lyrics to the song "See Me, Feel Me" from the show *Tommy*. The main repeated verse is "See me, feel me, touch me, heal me"! They wanted me to know who they are and what they think. They reached out to me for help in healing some of the wounds inflicted by social or cultural brainwashing. It was a chance to validate their whole being, not just whether they wanted to be parents.

Although I kept going back to questions about rejection, many of my correspondents seemed to exude a need to tell me how they decided on being childfree, their age, if they were married or not, what they did in their professions, or what they were doing for their education.

Most were very, very sure of their decision to remain childfree. Yet, they still wanted me to know them not as a rejected person, but as a human with warmth, feelings, and intelligence.

You'll see in some of my questions that I, too, wanted to know more about them than how they faced rejection. Where were they from? Who were they? Why did they reach out to me? Were they in relationships? How did their partners feel? When did they first feel they didn't want to parent? How did that feel to them? Did they ever tell anyone, or think they might change their minds?

This chapter contains ardent, sometimes shocking, and surprisingly inspiring revelations about being childfree in countries other than the United States. Some countries are more accepting. In others, sadly, childfree people are rejected with rage and contempt. Just like in America, people who live in larger cities seem to be more accepting of personal choices without condemnation. Those who live in more rural areas or religious communities tend to be harsher with people who defy the norms. So, when you read these voices calling out to you with sincere frankness, remember that you're seeing one reaction from one person in one area of one country. It may not represent the entire population. But how many other experiences are echoed in that one voice?

In some countries, your life may be at stake if you dare say you never want to have children. We all know the hideous stories of stoning women to death for dishonor to their families in Pakistan and other countries where Sharia Law is the rule. Many countries have awful punishments for women who don't want or can't have children.

Reading about people's loneliness may feel like a dagger in your stomach if you've had similar experiences. When you read about a professional Indian woman being treated as a bad omen to a friend's children, you may feel shock and anger. When you read about a Nigerian doctor who can't have a relationship until after she's passed menopause, you'll value your own loving partnerships and hold them closer to your heart. When you read about women who, if found to be infertile, suffer the indignity of knowing their mates can seek another woman, you may feel outrage! Hearing that infertile women are thought of as men, you'll cringe at the inhumanity. Knowing that a brilliant Greek woman is thought of as "soulless" may bother you. Learning that, years ago, women in Hungary were monitored to be sure they had full pregnancies and not abortions, you may shudder at the awfulness. In one country, it's a duty for a woman to give birth. I had no idea a woman from Slovakia knew about issues regarding Planned Parenthood and abortion! Finally, one woman fears the stigma of growing older without children, and being thought no more than a maid because of that.

As a retired teacher of ESL with so many diverse people in my classrooms, I've always been excited to learn about different cultures. I've also wanted to understand the role that cultural expectations play in choosing the childfree lifestyle.

There were times when I muddled through the challenges of speaking or writing in another language to the people I connected with for this chapter. My background in teaching English as a second language was a huge help. Many felt at ease knowing I was a teacher of English. They appreciated my familiarity with simple language and my comfort speaking slowly. I also know how to write in easily comprehensible English. In the excerpts that follow, I've corrected some of the grammar and spelling so my correspondents' writing is easier to read.

This writing journey took me down a path I had never traveled before, and demonstrated the need for more books on this subject written in other languages. Of course, we can't say whether other countries would allow a book categorized as "against the norm." I don't have that answer. I do know that many books I've sent to women in different countries were not received.

But it's not all bad news. Despite the rejection that many people feel, there are countries whose people and institutions are more open and accepting of personal lifestyle choices.

What follows are actual communications from childfree people in Argentina, Bulgaria, Russia, Spain, Hungary, Germany, Madagascar, Greece, St. Croix, Italy, India, Slovakia, the UK, and the continents of Australia and Africa.

You'll notice it was mainly women who communicated with me. That's not surprising, as it's only recently that men even in the U.S. have been more open and outspoken. I chose not to comment on each share. I believe their words will be enough.

Letter from Pablo in Argentina:
Hi Marcia,

I did have a little rejection from my family, at first. My father told me once, "You don't want children? You were a child yourself, you know?" A lot of people say this as if it was a valid argument. Children grow up and become independent and able to decide whether to have offspring or not. My mother told me several times that she wanted grandchildren, and my response could not be more eloquent: Ask my siblings! I don't like children. I won't have any.

My parents got used to the idea... eventually. Now it is perfectly natural for them. They realized (I suppose) that not everything in life is giving birth. In my case, I chose to live as I want, do as I want, without asking anyone if they like my lifestyle or not. I work, travel, attend cooking courses, study as many languages as I can, play video games, and I'm planning to play the piano sometime in the (not too distant, I hope) future.

My wife (well, we're not legally married, but we've been living together since 2003) dislikes children as much as I do, if not more. Her parents never complained about not having grandchildren. Their daughter is a successful bank businesswoman, and that's everything they needed.

Most of her co-workers have children. At first, they thought it was a little shocking that we decided not to have any. Furthermore, some of them found it almost insulting that we call our two cats "our sons." If there is something that I've learned over the years with these people, it's that you can't argue with a "breeder." Children are everything to them, the only purpose in life, and that's it. Waste of time arguing.

You said that some people have lost their families, friends, and even jobs for their decision against procreating. In Argentina, that is not the case. There may be some cases of discrimination against the childfree, but they are not the norm.

I hope I gave you a basic idea of our situation. If there is anything at all that you would like to know, please don't hesitate to ask me.

Cheers!

Pablo

Here's an eye-opening letter from Romania:

Dear Marcia,

First of all, yes, in Romania I can tell people that I do not want to have children. We have free speech, my country is democratic, a member of the European Union, but it is still one of the poorest countries in the EU, and had a dominant rural tradition until 1930-1940. The population is 90 percent orthodox and, not least, the country was incredibly delayed in its evolution by the communist regime that ruled the nation for forty-two years (1947-1989). It was a regime that developed urbanism, economy, and industry, but there was a huge price to pay for all these: rations (very little food, very few consumer durables, we had electricity only for a few hours per day, one single TV program that used to air only two hours per day, containing mostly communist propaganda)—dictatorship in one of its most ugly forms. The regime isolated Romania from the rest of Europe, the borders were closed, and the country survived on its own, due to its natural resources—but they required a labor force.

Labor force is a key concept. Through a combination of modernization of the Romanian community, high participation of women in the labor market, and a low standard of living, the number of births has significantly declined since the 1950s. However, the leaders saw the decreasing number of births mainly as a result of the decree issued in the late '50s that legalized abortion. To counter this sharp decline of the population, the Communist Party decided that the Romanian population should be increased by more than twenty-five million inhabitants. So, Ceausescu authorized the infamous Decree 770. Abortion and contraception were declared illegal.

To enforce the decree, society was strictly controlled. Contraceptives disappeared from the shelves and all women were forced to be monitored, monthly, by a gynecologist. Any detected pregnancies were followed until birth. Secret police kept a close eye on operations in hospitals. Sex education was refocused primarily on the benefits of motherhood, including the ostensible satisfaction of being a heroic mother who gives her homeland many children.

The direct consequence of the decree was a huge baby boom—children born out of fear, so many of them unwanted. During those awful decades, a large number of children ended up living in orphanages because their parents could not cope. Also, about ten thousand women died due to complications arising from illegal abortions performed at home. People without children and people who were not married were forced to pay double taxes to the state. Violence in the families was simply a part of life— and sadly it still is today.

We've had almost thirty years of democracy already, but tradition still imposes rudimentary attitudes and ways of thinking. Most people still believe that only mothers are women (at least declaratively, because in reality all women are still largely treated as objects—and the saddest part is that many women treat themselves and other women as objects, because they don't know any better).

In their holy hypocrisy (I just told you that most Romanians are orthodox), many people paradoxically have no shame about humiliating and judging those who are different. Women are still assigned roles by the society, by their families (including their own parents, sadly...). They are raised in a spirit that emphasizes motherhood and marriage as supreme achievements. If we go back to statistics once again (80 percent of Romanian families are abusive, a woman earns significantly less than a men, a woman suffers from domestic violence every thirty seconds, etc.) you may realize how twisted things actually are, even today. Freedom and democracy are such fragile concepts, believe me, and sometimes this thought terrifies me.

There are people who fight, there are people who stand for their life choices, as I do, but I cannot tell you how hard it is to live in such a context, which is so far from being appreciated for what you really are, as an individual. Very few people respect me for being childfree by choice and unmarried by choice. It almost doesn't matter that I am a woman with an academic foundation. It doesn't matter that I've lived with my man for twenty years now, and that we are just fine, and actually much, much better than most married people we know. I still have to deal with condescendence, with people rude enough to attempt to explain me that I am wrong, that I am selfish, etc., and I have a mother and a father for whom my life choices were always a disappointment. And I've always had to live with this, although nobody should have to live with this. Trust me. It kills you inside.

Well, I hope that I have made myself understood. The English language is a bit difficult for me, but ask me for any other details that you need to know and I will do my best to answer, okay? Hugs!

Laura

P.S. Oh, I realized that I didn't write you anything about why I think people have children in my country these days. Well, in most cases it's this global trend that fetishizes motherhood through the media. The kid is now a personal prize. Parents are still privileged, regardless of their qualities. Funny, most people who accuse me of being selfish, when they are asked "Why do you have kids?" their answer starts with "Because I need…"

Here's a revealing letter from India:

Dear Marcia,

I'm so sorry for the delay. I wanted to write with a peaceful mind rather than writing in hurry.

In my early teens, I was pretty determined not to have children. But there was a twist in the tale when I realized I was in love with my boyfriend. He proposed to me. I didn't say yes immediately. I was about twenty-two years old and studying physiotherapy. Guilt crawled into my mind that I shouldn't persuade a man to be childfree and deprive him of the joy of fatherhood. I started going through all the OB/GYN books in our huge central library to learn each and every fact about pregnancy and childbirth. I spent more time with my baby brother and watched my mom to learn child-rearing skills, trying to feel the joy she seemed to experience. I followed parenting columns in the newspapers. In every bit of my mind I wished that something would change my decision and I would crave to be a mom, as all my friends seemed to do. But, alas, my analytical brain had a different plan for me. So I wrote a long letter to my boyfriend clearly saying that I didn't want to become a mother. I suggested he could move on if he wished.

To my surprise and relief, he called to say that he is perfectly fine with my decision, and that he also is not willing to have children. He wants to spend his life with me only, and no third party should be tolerated. I was very happy and enjoyed almost six years of courtship. We married at the age of twenty-eight years.

My in-laws were furious that their son was marrying an old girl. In India, twenty-eight is considered "old" for marriage. They doubted whether I would be able to conceive and produce a healthy baby. Needless to say, we were very much settled on our life and completely ignored their protest.

The true struggle began after our marriage. All our close female relatives hinted that we should have a baby as soon as possible, since I was already twenty-eight and my biological clock was ticking.

We came to live in Mumbai, as my husband was working there, leaving my in-laws and parents in Kolkata. We thought people would not be able to interfere much in our life. We were wrong! One of my husband's aunts called him and whispered, "Don't allow your wife to take any contraceptive medicines. Let the first pregnancy happen as early as possible." (She considered at least two children mandatory.) My mother-in-law echoed the same thing every time we called her.

My mother hinted when she visited us that she was

eagerly waiting for at least one grandchild. My father and father-in-law didn't say anything directly, but they also dropped hints, like how their friends are becoming grandfathers now and enjoying their last few years of life with grandchildren. I always thought only women have the talent to emotionally blackmail someone. Our fathers proved me wrong!

Durga Puja, where Goddess Durga is worshipped, is the biggest festival of Bengali Hindus. This is the time all Bengalis living outside Bengal come home. It is a family reunion. Once, during this festival, in our temple during a social gathering, women asked me how many years we had been married and why we were not planning for children. In a gathering of ladies, one lady said to me, "Next Durga Puja, I want to see you three... not two." I felt rejected as a worthwhile woman in her eyes. I deflected queries and comments for four years. I told people we were very busy, but would think about it later. I couldn't face the rejection we knew would be aimed at us.

So, every year when we went home during Durga Puja, we were bombarded with questions from family and even strangers! When are we going to give the "good news," or how long will our family planning go on?

However, most of the people who are very professional in India don't show much interest in my personal life. They might have casually asked about children, but when I told them of my decision (I finally did tell them my decision) they were surprised but not shocked. So, the acceptance was more among the properly educated and creative people. It also depends on the type of society they are brought up in. Our senior administrator, though highly educated, has a conservative background. One day, I went to meet him for some official reason. He asked me casually how many children I planned to have. When I said zero, he immediately said, "I know a very good gynecologist. You can meet her with my reference." I stood there in shock and embarrassed. He never considered that I didn't want children. However, the emotional blackmail from friends, family, and co-workers continued.

Another well-known lady doctor (who is my colleague) said to me that I am going against nature. She said, "Our body is made to produce children. That balances the hormones in the female body." She warned that I would get diseases like breast cancer if I never bore a child. She implored me to understand that children are like insurance policies. She insisted that if we invest well in children with our time, the profit would be returned in the future. The insurance policy thing is a common concern among all my parents, relatives, friends, and whomever we met. All threatened us with a horrible old age when we will have no one to look after us and we will die like street dogs. Some mocked our "pseudo happiness." Some were really concerned about our personal properties, as we will not have any heir.

We stopped visiting my in-laws for two years, as the situation was really getting difficult. We hoped things would be better when my brother-in-law married. But the pressure increased. My mother-in-law one day called me and in a very strong, harsh voice said that she wants a grandchild by hook or crook. I was furious hearing that, and told my husband that it was time we told the truth. So, my husband declared that we don't want to have children, though we are very much capable of having them. That was a very new and shocking concept for them.

They refused to believe it and straightaway blamed me for sowing such thoughts in his head.

My parents also were shocked but they laughed it off, saying we will change our minds in the future. Still, both families feel we are making a colossal blunder by not having babies. Neighbors don't mingle with us! I think they have the idea that I am infertile, which is called "banj" in Hindi. They keep their children a safe distance from me, as if their children could catch this affliction. Marcia, do you want to talk about rejection?

Some of the people who know may be jealous of our lifestyle. We live in a two-bedroom apartment and own a car, while they live in a one-bedroom with three to four people together. We travel a lot, have late-night parties, and go out to dinner in lovely restaurants. Our comfort and exciting lifestyle may be an eyesore to them.

We are now going through a phase where we have learned to ignore all of them and live our own lives. But I still feel somewhat uneasy with all the nasty questions and the attempts to insult us for not having children. My parents may feel the wrath, as they may be shunned for having a daughter such as me!

I hope this serves your purpose. Rejection, in India, is common if you say you don't want children. Though I have not seen you or met you or heard your voice, still I feel a deep connection with you.

I don't know why or how! Whenever I'm feeling low regarding this decision, knowing you're there to reach on the Internet cheers me up. Marcia, you don't know how you inspire this Indian lady thousands and thousands of miles away from you. I'm very lucky and thankful.

Love,

Chatterjee

A letter from Germany:
Hello Marcia,

I'm a thirty-four-year-old German woman. I want to tell you about the situation in my country concerning childfree people. Since Germany is one of the most developed countries in the world, with excellent access to birth control, I suppose it's one of the easiest places to live when you do not want to have children. A second positive point is the relatively slight influence of religious communities, which seems to be very strong in lots of American communities. It's not very noticeable here. Those who adhere to a religious community mostly remain among themselves and do not interfere with other peoples' lives. Since I live in the center of a medium-size city, I have little contact with neighbors. The chances of being observed and commented on are very slim. My circle of friends contains quite a few childless or single people. The same goes for my partner's circle of friends. I don't have many friends who have children.

Now I come to the not-so-positive side. One thing is the attempt by our state to increase our birth rate. In that respect, overpopulation doesn't seem to be a point politicians or parties would ever bring up. The tendency is to consider the future of our country threatened by too few children. We have a retirement system that was introduced at the end of the eighteenth century, which strongly builds on younger generations working to pay the older generations' retirement. The trouble with this system is that it depends on an ever-growing society, which makes it not only unfit, but, in my opinion, immoral for the future of our planet. It still works as an excellent argument when it comes to supporting families and increasing our country's birth rate—in short: praising reproduction. The attempt to do so works mainly via payments made to families such as a substitute income when you leave work for one year and tax breaks for children. It hasn't had a real effect on the country's birth rate yet. The reason might be that many mothers struggle with the double role of being a mother and a working woman at the same time. Finding childcare is a daunting task! So, to relate back to the point of not having children in Germany, a very common argument is that not having children means you did not pay your dues to our society, or more bluntly: who is going to pay for your pension? In the worst cases, some people claim that childless people should not get any retirement pay. This is the most common argument I've heard in my country. And this is often also a reason parents give when asked why they *had* children. You can see why I don't share my choice to remain childfree! I don't want the rejection or sermons about my duty to the country!

When I asked a former co-worker whether she wanted children, she replied with: "Of course. This is the first and foremost duty of a citizen." I have to say that at work there are some female co-workers who just keep presuming that at some point I'm going to have children. I don't think it is something they mean badly. It's simply a sign that we do have many people who just presume that one follows the general life script. It is only very close friends to whom I open up and clearly state that I do not want children. It is a private decision, and the conversations that follow are normally not the most relaxing and enjoyable ones. The feeling of rejection is not pleasant! Why go there?

My relationship to my mother would be closer if I knew that she would accept my decisions and me as I am! I do feel some sort of selfishness is behind her trying to talk me into having children. I really hope my brother will compensate this for her. He doesn't seem to be against having children.

Kind regards, and lots of power and inspiration for your work!

Love,

Monika

A letter from Australia:

I am a thirty-four-year-old woman living in an individualist culture in Australia, but I grew up in a Chinese household, which meant that there was a high level of collectivism. This was difficult to navigate during my youth, and continues to shape my identity as an Asian female who was born and grew up in Australia.

The topic of being childfree has really only recently gained momentum in Australia. There are more stories of women being childfree and programs on television such as *Insight* which discuss the issue. I think it comes as part of a wave of female-centric topics: wage inequality, reproductive rights, domestic violence, balancing work and home life. Ultimately, motherhood and the very definition of what it means to be a woman often plagues my mind. I am grateful that I live in Australia, where generally you can decide if you want to be a parent or not, but it is not without stigma. Whilst it is probably a bit better than being in China, I still feel that women are almost conditioned to take the path of motherhood.

We had policies in Australia where if you had a child you were given a "baby bonus. I'm not sure what the amount was, I think it was about $2,000, and our previous treasurer once encouraged women to "Have a baby for mum, a baby for dad, and a baby for the country." How pronatalist can it get? I think this all happened back in the late 2000s, so I had just graduated from university. I must admit I've probably been subconsciously childfree since I was an adolescent, but I really started to think about being childfree once I started full-time work. At university, I was really just concentrating on my studies and dating. Marriage and children were the furthest things from my mind. I think as I got older and gained more confidence and read up on feminism, as well as really set aside time to understand my family and the relationship dynamics, I was heading toward a childfree lifestyle anyway. When I started dating my now husband, we had to have this discussion again, as when people start dating, family and friends are naturally curious about our plans. I must admit that the biggest issue I have with being childfree is tolerating the judgment and rejection, particularly from family members. It is even worse in a family-centric culture. I've always been one to question choices and I have had many arguments with my family about whether having kids was worth it. However, it is still difficult to be in a minority. You don't want to tell people why you don't think parenthood will happen for you, but it gets asked about in social gatherings. I've had a lot of people say I might change my mind (it has been about twenty years, and I am still not keen) or be outright rude and say that it is strange, selfish, unnatural. My own mother has said such things, which is why I tend to keep it to myself. There is the judgment about how your life is not meaningful without kids, how you are too career-driven or materialistic. I've even read that some people think we are "freeloaders," as we have decided to take a path that does not contribute to the economy or society as much as parents. The truth is I just don't really have the urge or the temperament to be a mother. I had to be realistic also: did we have the resources to raise a child in an increasingly expensive city such as Sydney where Gen Y can barely afford a home? And yes, I admit, my dream of one day traveling the world with my husband for a year or two also plays a part. I am a feminist at heart, and it pains me to see women still being judged on the life choices they make. I contrast that with my husband, who rarely gets asked questions about kids. Perhaps because people automatically assume womanhood = motherhood, I don't know. I wish people, especially women, weren't defined by whether or not they had kids. Perhaps over time I will get more confident saying it out loud, but at the moment only a few friends and my family know that I am not keen on this path. I feel like as an adult individual I don't need to justify my choices, particularly to strangers, which is often what it feels like when people find out you don't have kids.

Sincerely,

Stephanie Lee

A letter from Slovakia:

My name is Nikoleta. I am from Slovakia. I am twenty-five. I'm childfree with a partner who also does not want kids.

What really saddens me is the humiliation we get for choosing to be childfree. We are viewed as betrayers of womanhood, betrayers of bloodline and humanity. People can get so defensive and so nasty with the comments. I am blessed to have an understanding family... well, except my mother. When she heard about my choice, she got super emotional and angry... because it's all about her, not me. What about her grandchildren and how selfish I am? She's not thinking.

At this time, I make enough to live happily with my partner. If I had a child, I would need to give up my job, be in constant fear for my health, and damn sure my relationship would be lost. It would take too much from us to get through the whole process. Also, I am vegan, and society is not prepared to not stick its nose in how do you raise a person even if it's healthy, never mind the two hundred comments about how you have to raise a child and how you do it wrong. I can't imagine getting more shit just because I refuse animal products, and so would my child, if I had any.

I am following a Slovakian vegan blogger. She also made a video about why she doesn't want kids, emphasizing the carbon footprint on the planet and 150 million un-adopted children around the world. "Shouldn't breeding really be the question?" she asked. Oh the backlash she had here! Most said she was a disgrace for supporting women who do not give a child to this world. People wrote that we, the childfree, should be stripped of rights, because we are not contributing enough to this world. We aren't sacrificing enough for humanity. We will die out and such.

I am proudly childfree. I speak loudly about my willingness to get my tubes removed. It saddens me that we are told that we can be whatever we want to be... until we reach a certain point... then we are expected to give up on our life and bear a child... or we failed as a woman?

Society scares me. And what's happening in America with the American health care plan with regards to Planned Parenthood and abortions. I look to America for wisdom. It's frightening to see how things are changing in your county, and how my uterus is other people's concern and people are getting charged for abortion even if it's a rape... this world is disgusting for me and I am glad I chose to get sterilized before these stupid laws reach my country.

Even in Poland, abortion is illegal, so there are buses that will bring girls and woman to Slovakia or Czechia for the surgery. Many of my friends are so afraid. I always had this image of America and women's rights. When I hear that abortion facilities in America are under attack by the government and shutting down, I feel frightened. And those guys want to control a woman's uterus so bad. I am scared we will take that example and it will influence Europe in a bad way if it passes, which I hope it won't!

I am so glad for your Facebook group! I feel more confident. I just hope I will be like you when I will grow up. You are a big inspiration for everyone who feels like a freak, or broken by society. We need to make this heard. This is not a taboo. We have a right to a happy life too.

Sincerely,
Nikoleta

A letter from Ksenia, a Russian living in Spain:

Being childfree in Russia is much harder than in Spain. Being European and in some aspects a very progressive country, Spanish people are more lax about church, marriage, and children. Many friends of ours are single, gay, childfree, have children but aren't married, etc. This may be normal in big cosmopolitan cities like Barcelona or Madrid, but smaller inland areas are more conservative and place more importance on traditional values and customs. They often go to church on Sundays, and therefore follow church sermons about family, women's role in the family, and of course children. In Russia, there is also a lot of church influence lately, but because natal-centered policies from the government use the church as a tool. Government is preoccupied with population decline and tries to raise the birth rate, on one hand, by offering monetary compensation for second and third children. On the other hand, by brainwashing! So many men and women really think that a woman who hasn't given birth is not a woman at all, that abortion is murder of an innocent child (although, at least for now, it is legal), that women should do everything possible to keep their husbands happy, stay at home, and raise children. Very sexist, in my opinion. Women still go to the university and work, but many expect to find a man, have a couple of children, and stay home for several years (maternity leave is one and a half years paid and up to four and a half years unpaid). I heard some university students complaining that their teachers told them not to worry about final exams, because they would not really need the degree since they should get married and stay at home with children. So pregnant women and young mothers steadily become sacred cows and, adding this social treatment to the lack of manners and education that some have, pregnancy came to mean that everybody is in debt to them and they can behave in aggressive and demanding ways. There is even a name for them among the childfree:

ovulators. We say they have ovulated their brain away. Of course, not all are this way, but many more than ever before. So, "He's just a kid, let him do what he wants" excuses started to be heard a lot when anyone complains about kids' behavior. If you write in a forum that you have doubts about having children, the responses are very aggressive and threatening. They may wish you death or suffering, since you are obviously insane. Among my own family and friends from Russia, the most frequent question is, "When are you going to have kids?" That also happens in Spain, but much less frequently. And the reactions when I say "never" are normally of disbelief. They try to persuade me I 'm still too young and will change my mind. On the other side, under so much pressure, many young women and men in Russia adopt the contrary position and become child haters. Many teenagers are also very rude and aggressive (with language) with kids, pregnant women, or mothers and claim they are CH (child haters). Because of these young people with such radical views and bad manners, normal childfree people have bad reputations. But none of this really made me become childfree. In fact, just a year ago I thought I wanted children. I read books about pregnancy, talked about kids with my husband and my family, and everybody was very sure that soon we would have kids. The day I turned thirty (that has been considered the appropriate age for us to start trying), I realized I wanted to carry on studying, and children would not allow that. So I cried a lot and wished I was a man. I had a big dissonance between what I thought I wanted and what I really wanted, and finally told my husband I didn't want children. I understood that in fact I don't even like children, which I'd tried to hide until then. But I do love animals, and I have them, and I never question myself about whether I really wanted them or not, because it was crystal clear for me, as it wasn't about children. What helped me to make up my mind was feminism and some Russian childfree forums where I could see people behaving in different ways than society expected them to behave. My husband at the beginning was shocked. He did not reject me at any moment, but he found it difficult to process. After some weeks, he started to understand my point of view and to feel sympathy for it, too. Now we feel completely okay with this idea and happy about it. However, I did go to a psychologist at the beginning because I found it hard to accept that I was "different," and I had big internal conflicts. The solution for these conflicts was to accept that I do know for sure that I don't want children right now, but I can't tell whether ten years from now I won't. Although I feel I won't, not having limits and having a choice feels much better.

Ksenia

I thanked her for this letter. She responded:

No need for thanking, since I just wanted to express my feelings and reflections to somebody who would understand my view. You are the right person. I wish I had more people to speak with here. I am grateful that you are so accessible. For me it is important to know childfree people of different ages, not only young ones, and learn from their experience, in large part because of all the fears that society tries to instill in us about getting old without children. "Who is going to bring you a glass of water once you are old?" is a typical question that people ask us. And it's amazing to know people who love their lives as they are and enjoy every day at any age!

A letter from Irena in Bulgaria:

I will just explain things. Bulgaria is a small country next to the Black Sea. It was not very well developed until recent times. My mother is Russian and her family was and remains very religious. Anyway, the point is that people from the previous generation still have the mindset that one must have kids. According to my mother, I have no other life purpose than to have children. I am a big disappointment for her. That really hurts me so much. That rejection goes right to my heart. I am a caring person, I have many animals, but I really am not keen on children and never was.

It is *not* socially accepted here to not have kids. It is taboo to say out loud that one doesn't like or want kids. It automatically means you are a bad person. As I mentioned before, even my mother disapproves, and when she goes to church she always prays for me to have children, even though she is fully aware I do not want any. This is a topic we discuss all the time with each other. For so many years she simply could not accept that I am not having kids. She thinks I will have no meaning in my life. When I try to reason with her by telling her, for example, that kids are expensive, that I have a career and I feel good about myself, she says that even if I don't have money for kids, I should have one, because my child might become very famous or smart. Imagine that? Anyway, she says, "You just give birth and faith will show the way." For people from the previous generation, or very religious people, reasoning doesn't work. They are blind to personal choice.

So, as you can imagine, we don't get along, because every time I see her she just talks about that and says I am a failure because I haven't given birth.

It is not socially accepted to not have kids. Everyone is asking why I still don't have any. When I say I prefer not to, I get the usual "Oh, but you will love it" and how happy I will be. I have tried to reason with people, telling them stories about postpartum depression, men leaving women, women blaming their kids for their lost years, and that I don't think I have enough money to provide a proper upbringing! No one listens. They just repeat and repeat that I have to. I hear this even from women who I know are unhappy parents! It's like a social mantra, everyone repeats the same thing, not giving a shred of thought to what they say.

I have tried so many different approaches to explaining, as I hope to make people understand that having children is not a requirement, but a matter of choice. None of them were convinced!

I am not always outspoken about it because, as I said, one is perceived as a bad person if they don't wish to have children. People who already have children are offended because somehow they see my personal choice as a threat to their decisions. It's not a good idea to talk about how good it is to not have children in front of people who already have them.

In sum, across Europe, the highly educated, the religiously uncommitted, and those who value autonomy are much more likely to approve of voluntary childlessness. Here, I am considered a rejected failure!

Irena

From Angela, age forty-six, in Italy:

This is a very religious country. The pope lives here! Most people assume their goals in life are to marry and start a family.

At five years old, I told my mom I never wanted to be a mom. She told me I would change my mind. I never did. I have no regrets. My parents have disowned me. However, it may be much easier to have one or two children (most parents don't have more than this) in my small town in Italy. Everyone seems to help. There's a spirit of reaching out and caring. In the evenings, it's not unheard of to see adults dining at 10 p.m. with a baby in their carriage. Children who are older have respect for being polite in public places. I'm shocked at the posts I read about kids in America screaming or not listening to parents.

I'm a total reject to the people in my town. I never had kids and wear clothes that I want to and not just because it's allowed in any season. (Here, if you wear shorts and cooler tops before a certain summer date, it's unacceptable. It doesn't matter if it's terribly hot! It's not accepted.) I constantly hear buzzing behind my back or snickering at the grocery store or while dining out with my husband. I don't care! I go home to my childfree lifestyle and laugh! I'm sure people think I'm going straight to hell. (I don't believe in any organized religion, either!)

I see too many of my women friend assuming the role of mother even though they also may have careers. They still must keep it all together, have Sunday dinners with the family, including their parents, and do too much for their children. This was not for me. Still isn't, and I'm thankful I never took on the traditional role. Instead, I take in abandoned animals that are often rejected after a baby arrives.

Angela

Next we hear from a woman in Nigeria. We communicated through private messages on the Internet. I've changed her name to protect her reputation. Yes, her reputation as a doctor would be tarnished if people knew her truth, even though she tells her close friends and family she never wants to have or raise children of her own.

"I want you to write my words" she messaged me. "Because I would want other Nigerian women to know it is an option to not procreate!"

Inori Ogbu: I tell people I never want children when it comes up in conversation with my friends or family. Because of my age people tend to ask me all the time! I am thirty-eight.

They usually say I will regret it, or ask who will take care of me when I am old, or say that having children will make me so happy. They are sure I will be a great mother! I really don't care about the rejection because I am not prepared to put my life on hold because of children who may or may not turn out okay. Because of my personality, I tend not to get many arguments from people trying to convince me.

Even Nigerians living abroad have a relative (usually the mother) come to stay for as long as is allowed to look after the baby.

Me: How can poor Nigerians afford to have children? Is abortion allowed? Can they get morning-after pills?

How's infertility viewed? Can a man divorce because of that?

Inori Ogbu: Most can't afford to have children. Most are poor. So they end up sending their children to live with wealthier relatives or strangers in urban areas who pay for their schooling or apprenticeship in exchange for them doing household chores and looking after the kids.

Abortion is very illegal in Nigeria, but still very much performed undercover.

Morning-after meds are over-the-counter in pharmacies! The only obstacle to getting them would be lack of knowledge that they exist, what they do, how to use them, or funds.

Infertility? The attitude to infertility is one of pity. Women are called "men" if they cannot have children, and are made fun of. For example, my mother is called Mama Inori. Her title is honored through my given name.

So, if a woman has no children, she remains nameless! See what I mean? I don't have to worry about that because there's still hope I can have a child in the future.

Me: What? Women are called "men" if they don't or can't reproduce? How awful for those women!

Inori Ogbu: Men definitely divorce women for infertility. That is why there is so much pressure to have children; otherwise he may marry a second wife. Polygamy is allowed in most places, or men can have kids outside of the marriage.

Then there is the need to have a male child. So, even when you have kids, you need to have a boy as well.

Me: Have you chosen to marry?

Inori Ogbu: I am a public health doctor. I travel a lot. I am not married because I have not found anyone who I believe is ready to be childfree, and I do not want any pressure.

I am waiting for when it's physically impossible.

Me: What is the role of a public health doctor? Also, if people assume you don't have children because you're not married, are you safer that way in your profession?

Inori Ogbu: I provide medical care in rural areas of Nigeria. I am involved with developing programs that deal with reproductive health and child health. Yes, I am safer because I am not married.

Me: I'm so proud of you! You can help many who don't know what you know. You make me smile knowing you are there. I wish I could go through this computer and give you a hug, if you allowed that!

Inori Ogbu: I wish that too. Here, I feel alone. Knowing you're there is comforting. Too many women don't know this is a good choice.

The next share was a lengthy conversation via private messages on the Internet. Later we decided to Skype, where I met Wendy's husband, Clint.

From Wendy in St. Croix, U.S. Virgin Islands:

Since it's a U.S. territory, there are a lot of transplants here, but most of them are either empty-nesters or younger people who are either very adventurous or childfree like us. While I feel like people on the mainland tend to revolve their lives around their children, the younger transplants that have kids here seem to be living the lives they want to lead and integrating their kids into their lives.

While on the mainland it's hard to get together with friends who have little kids, there's a much more vibrant social life here. The people we hang out with are more dog-oriented, which we love.

In terms of the locals, they're really laid back. Everybody leads their own lives and respects everyone else's choices. I feel a lot less judged here, for sure.

Back in Iowa, where I'm from, the conversation tends to turn to kids within the first minute. If you don't have kids it's like the other person doesn't really know how to connect with you anymore. Whereas here, it seems completely expected that people can and will have an identity and life outside of children.

I stopped the instant messaging here and asked to Skype. Here's more of what I learned from Wendy and her husband Clint. After reading the notes from our conversations, you may want to pack your bags and head to St. Croix!

Wendy and Clint were born and raised in Iowa. They're in their thirties. Both assumed they would follow a life script Wendy described as, "You know... marriage, a house, career, and kids." Her sweet face didn't have the sunbathed look I expected from life on St. Croix. Maybe that's because she works as an academic adviser and not as a surfing instructor, as I'd imaged. Silly me! Her husband, Clint, sat next to her and introduced me to their two dogs. I, in turn, introduced them to my Chihuahua. The beauty of Skype is the ability to get more details through questioning. Clint is very loquacious with a warm smile and a slightly receding hairline. Clint had no job waiting for him when they packed the house they'd built with four bedrooms to house kids and headed to this magical island, where Wendy had a lucrative dream career as an academic adviser.

"Did you get a lot of pressure to have kids in Iowa?" I asked them.

Although I saw Wendy open her mouth, Clint was the first to respond: "We sure did. But we told our friends and family we had a BBB list we had to accomplish first. That's a Before Baby Bucket list!"

I smiled at Clint's need to share first. Men have so much to say, don't they? We underestimate how much this lifestyle affects them.

I asked if people wanted to know when the BBB list was done, because wouldn't that mean babies are next? They both nodded and smiled at each other. Clint rolled his eyes as he nodded in confirmation. He explained that when Wendy was offered the job in St. Croix, they realized they never wanted to have kids at all! "If we had them, we never would have been able to move to St. Croix!" Wendy said with a giggle.

"So," I asked, "are there different attitudes toward having or not having kids in St. Croix?

Wendy explained that on St. Croix, there's less of a keeping-up-with-the-Joneses mentality than stateside. The average vehicle is at least ten years old. Culturally, they're about thirty to forty years behind the U.S. mainland. Women are still the caretakers of children. Men have kids as a macho thing. Clint was quick to interject, "It's not uncommon for a man to have dozens of children from different women! Sadly, they don't help those children, but boast about how many kids they've fathered. Nobody goes after them to support their children! Families pitch in."

Wendy explained that people in St. Croix have many

identities other than parent. They embrace the arts, food, and hobbies, and never seem to be "bored" with or without kids.

I asked if they ever feel rejected for not having children. Wendy was quick to respond: "Nobody seems to care! It's almost like it's not polite to ask. They may assume we *can't* have kids."

Both Clint and Wendy taught me that conservatism on St. Croix shows itself in not baring too much skin, protecting privacy, and the Rastafarian faith, which, in Clint's definition, means, "Don't be a dick! Be helpful! Be respectful! Everyone is different."

When I researched Rastafarian beliefs, I learned that emphasis is placed on the idea that personal experiences and intuitive understanding should be used to determine the truth or validity of one's belief or practice. This may explain why the people on St. Croix allow for privacy in personal choices.

Before you pack your bags, they also told me their water cistern had a leak and they have had no water for four days. "It won't be fixed till Friday, if we're lucky," Wendy said. "I can't imagine how we could survive this if we had kids! Thank God we have only two dogs!"

I interviewed Linda Wilson, of Manchester, England, via Skype.

After a few attempts, we successfully saw each other's faces. The reaction, for me, was instantaneous. I wanted to reach out and hug her. Her smile was genuine. Something about her exuded warmth and a calm demeanor. Her eyes were very blue. Her face was cherubic, with long blond hair cascading down to a crisp white blouse.

I asked if I could use her real name, since so many people request that I not. She said, "Of course!"

Linda is a forty-three-year-young widow. (I know! So young to be a widow.) In fact, her beloved husband had died only three months before we spoke. Her eyes filled with tears when she shared that fact with me. He was older than her when they married. Although he had two grown children from a previous marriage, he never asked her to consider having a child with him. She was relieved!

Her first comment, after a few words of introduction and welcome, caught me off guard.

Linda: Do you know, here in the UK I've never heard the word "childfree"? Everyone says "childless."

Me: That's a new fact for me. How do you feel about the new word?

Her face lit up with a lovely smile.

Linda: I get it! I like it. It's a more enjoyable word than childless. I've never felt like less of anything.

Me: Then why *isn't* it used there?

Linda: Maybe there's no need for it here! "Childless" isn't a dirty word. Nobody cares if it's by choice or by fate. Nobody questions if you don't have kids. Maybe, from what I've seen on the childfree sites in America, it's more necessary there? Americans seem to be more defensive and require validation or feel more defensive about the pressure they get to procreate.

I chuckled, as she was right. Many childfree people are terribly defensive and even bordering on rude toward people who choose to have children. That usually stops after they come to see their own choice as perfectly okay.

Me: Did you ever think about having children as a

child?

Linda: I don't remember ever wanting children. If I told anyone, I would hear, "Oh, you're too young. You'll change your mind when you fall in love." When I fell in love at twenty-nine, I didn't have that mothering-children feeling, even though I loved him with all my heart. I do remember thinking maybe I wasn't normal! But, he was totally okay without us having children together, so I let that thought happily go.

Me: I'm wondering why you wanted to come to my Facebook site.

Linda: I heard that word "childfree" and was curious about learning more from others. So I researched with that word on Facebook. Remember, here I only knew "childless."

She giggled.

Me: So? What did you learn?

Linda: I was surprised to see so many angry, bitter, defensive people. Here, I never felt that way. There were other sites I finally left because I couldn't take the awful attitudes toward those who want kids, or the words like "crotch droppings" that I thought were unnecessary. I liked your site because it was more supportive, inviting, and accepting.

I told her how my administrators and I often had to block the kinds of things she'd seen on other sites.

Me: Do your friends have children?

Linda: Absolutely! But none of them pressure me or even questioned me about not having children. I think they think we couldn't have them! And I often wanted to say, "Don't feel sorry for me!" Here, most people aren't very nosey about personal things. I'm rarely asked what I do or who I live with.

Me: Well, that's not the way it is in America!

We both laughed together.

Linda shared that she works with mental health charities that she and her late husband were active in. She's met many unhappy parents. Some of them suffer from intense anxiety about raising their children.

Me: Do you think many people have kids due to religious pressures?

Her answer shocked me.

Linda: Not at all. Here, there's no push to "go forth and multiply," although maybe a bit more in the Catholic religion. I think the lessons of living by the Golden Rule are taught more than the need to procreate.

Me: Are there any courses in schools that question people's preparation to parent, or show any of the raw realities of raising kids?

Linda: Nope! Maybe one or two schools have those programed dolls, but they are in the minority.

She became a bit more serious with her next remark.

Linda: Here, there's a lot of child abuse! Parents see that it's hard work and they can't put them back! Many aren't suited to it, or have them too young. It's a sad reflection of how much we do need education on the parenting role.

I interviewed Betty Kaklamanidou, of Greece, via Skype. Betty has a PhD and works as an assistant professor of film and television theory and history at Aristotle University in Thessaloniki.

It was amazing to see the faces of Betty and her husband, Petros, on Skype. There I was, communicating with two people in Greece from my office. It brought back lovely memories of a cruise to those gorgeous Greek islands when I was in my thirties.

Betty's forehead was sweating slightly. She had a cigarette dangling from her mouth. She immediately explained how hot it was there, and that they kept the air-conditioning low to keep the air more "pure." I don't quite get that, but it's okay. I yelled at her for smoking.

Betty: Oh, you Americans! You always talk about what's right or wrong with smoking. It's my body. My life. Just like I never want to have kids! My choice. Stop with the threats of cancer. Many people smoke for a long life and die from something else!

I knew I was in for an adventure with Betty. She had spunk and bravado, yet she exuded warmth touched with humor.

Betty went from one topic to another with a relish to share her Greek culture. I knew she wanted someone to listen to her! I don't think she ever gets a chance in Greece, especially when it comes to not wanting children.

Me: How do you describe yourself?

Betty: A proud forty-five-year-old "scholar."

She looked at her husband and they both laughed.

Me: Did you ever want or think about having children?

Betty: Never wanted children. But when I met Petros in my early thirties I had a dilemma. He wanted kids! I guess I was lucky. I never was able to conceive. I finally announced to Petros that I didn't want children. He understood. We've been happily together without children for thirteen years.

She told me she wanted to read books on this subject to learn about other people who choose not to have children. I didn't ask, but maybe she had some guilt or a need to feel validated? Then again, she appears to be very, very confident and happy in her choice.

Betty: There are no books on the childfree lifestyle in Greece. Motherhood is sanctified here. I grew up watching *Little House on the Prairie*. I thought all families get along and solve problems in a half hour. I found out it's a lie.

Me: That TV show depicted an ideal family working and playing together on a farm in America.

Betty: There's no greater propaganda than Hollywood! But I loved it. My family was dysfunctional. I loved watching a family that seemed to work. However, it never made me want to have kids of my own.

Me: That kind of show is called a pronatalist show. We still have many TV shows trying to convince us that parenting is a fulfilling experience. Now they have more reality shows, but the result is usually the same. No matter what happens, children are the joy of life.

We both had a good laugh, with Petros joining us.

Me: What rejection have you endured for not having children?

Betty: I've been stigmatized as a childfree woman, even accused of being a mean, "soul-less" person by a female colleague who has children. I believe I'm also silently criticized by "friends" as actually wanting kids but never achieving fertilization.

She said the word "friends" while mimicking quotation marks with her fingers.

Betty: I was surprised to hear my mom admit she never wanted to have kids! Although it might have bothered some people to hear this from their own mom, for me, it validated my own choice! She was an awesome mom!

Me: You're lucky to have that feeling. I also know what that's like. Betty, do you think Greece is accepting of reproductive choices, or not?

Betty: In Greece, you have to have children!

She said this with great dramatic assertion. Her eyes were wide. Her voice was loud.

The last thing I asked was about her name.

Me: I'm wondering about your name. It's so old-American.

Her response made me chuckle.

Betty: It's really Despina.

After we said goodbye, I looked up "Despina." In Greek, it refers to "lady," but most of the time it's associated with the Virgin Mary! I wonder if she knew that?

I interviewed Lalina, in Madagascar, via instant message:

Lalina: Well, here, having kids is definitely a must. You're considered a woman who has less value if you are "childless." I keep telling my parents I'm never having kids. Once, my mum replied, "Don't ever repeat this. People will think you're crazy." I could barely speak, feeling totally rejected and placed into silence. I wanted her to hug me and say, "You're fine just the way you are. I love you." Not going to happen.

Me: You're fine just the way you are! I admire you very much.

Lalina: Thanks, Marcia.

Me: What about religion there? Does that influence the push to have a child?

Lalina: Ninety-nine percent of people here are "Christians," and thus they have to "be fruitful." And they're totally against abortion! They're easily shocked when they see on the news that a woman had an abortion. And if they could, they would kill the woman.

Me: Really? Kill?

Lalina: Absolutely. Can you imagine living with that fear?

Me: No. I can't!

Lalina: My parents think I *will* change my mind. But I won't. The battle will be hard, but with the life we're living here, the best way to protect children is not having any.

Me: What do you mean?

Lalina: We have bad leaders (greedy and corrupt) and bad people too. Currently they have practiced mob justice (yes!) when they caught red-handed someone who did something wrong. Would I be subjected to that if I were outspoken about not wanting children?

The level of insecurity is damn high. Yet people keep breeding!

Me: How are you different from the majority?

Lalina: What makes me different from the others is that I think a lot. I overthink. I ask questions in all situations and analyze things. That ruins my life sometimes, but I just can't help overthinking about everything.

Another reason why I don't want to have kids is that I think my life will be over once I have them. I will have to take care of them for the rest of my life. This scenario is just unbearable for me.

Me: What do you fear the most?

Lalina: Rejection! And death if anyone knows my

truth. You know what? I haven't been in a relationship since 2009. I consider it a waste of time with someone who sees you as a potential breeding machine. My insecurity about ever finding a life partner plagues me.

Insecurity is not the only issue here. In three words, "We are poor!" And I still don't get why people still want to have kids.

Me: Being challenged with money, you're wise not to have children.

Lalina: Actually, only my parents know I'm not having kids. But I've an aunt (from my father) who is childless. She's married, but treated like a maid. I guess if someday I get married, the same would happen to me!

Me: I doubt you would allow that, Lalina!

These communications show the universal reaction to being rejected over a personal choice. They prove this is a worldwide challenge creating far-reaching heartache for many wonderful people who are labeled, without justification, as worthless. They also show how some people face rejection without allowing it to make them its victim! Clearly, some countries may be more open about this lifestyle.

It's apparent that childfree people worldwide can lead exemplary lives, like that doctor in Nigeria. She wants to inform more women about birth control! Pablo from Argentina is the CEO of a company, helping others through his business and giving jobs to people raising children! The woman from Italy told me she takes in animals that are abandoned when people have children and can no longer take care of their pets. Ksenia said, "Activism is probably my meaning of life. I try to open my

189

mind, enhance intelligence, and expand understanding and transmit to others what I learn." Linda is active in charities in the UK. Are these people—or you, my reader—less than those who are parents?

I'm forever connected to all those who shared their stories with me. The many people I couldn't include, because it would take an entire book, have my gratitude for what they taught me.

My purpose is to help this lifestyle be seen as the beautiful choice it is. The childfree lifestyle is limited only by what you want. Some may want to nurture through causes. Travel may lure others. There's nothing wrong with those who simply want to nurture themselves. But nobody should feel the pain of rejection. Sadly, it's an international experience.

Chapter 10
Rejection from Within

"The lady doth protest too much, methinks."
—William Shakespeare, *Hamlet*

Every morning, I go to my six childfree support pages on Facebook to see what people are sharing. Sometimes I comment, validate, or simply "like" what people are sharing. Other times, I post an interesting article that may spur my followers to comment or vent. I often pose a question to explore differences and similarities of opinions. I'm always in awe of how many people still need the ongoing support we give and receive from each other. I sigh when I think of how many times I've heard, "But childfree people are accepted now! You don't need these sites."

If only that were true. My six Facebook sites, Instagram, and blog have more than ten thousand followers from all over the world. These sites continue to grow as more people find me on the Internet. Once they're welcomed and validated, it's as if a huge burden has been lifted. I've seen comments like, "You have no idea how much I needed this Facebook group. I thought I was the only one on this planet not wanting kids! It's refreshing to know I don't have to defend my choice!"

One morning, I opened my computer to find an email from one of my Facebook moderators. Having moderators is a huge help to me. Tending to six pages, Instagram, my blog, and other writing can be time-consuming. Knowing I have five special people watching and making sure things are going well is reassuring, especially if I can't check every day. One moderator wrote, "Marcia! Go to the closed site! There's an uprising. I'm concerned. Don't know how to handle it."

(A closed Facebook page is one where my moderators or I must accept you into it. There are required questions and a check of personal Facebook pages to rule out trolls or people there to stir the pot. It's a safer place to speak your truths, because it's not shared elsewhere, unlike an open page.)

I opened that page and found an impassioned post from a woman who was childfree by choice. She'd sought medical help when she wasn't feeling well. That led to tests proving she was five to six months pregnant. (This isn't unusual, as I've learned from Internet research and seen on TV shows featuring obese women.) Her anguished lament was, "How did this happen? I was on birth-control pills! He had a vasectomy!" Her post was met with sympathy by people who suggested an abortion. When she told everyone it was too late for that, they suggested giving the child up for adoption, since many people facing infertility could make loving parents. The majority of people were sympathetic and told her they felt empathy for her and the horror she was now facing.

However, there were others who were angry, annoyed, and downright verbally abusive. Their comments were:

"Seriously? You two really had birth control? Obviously, someone didn't!"

"Your partner is lying! He probably never had a vasectomy!"

"Um. Maybe you screwed another man?"

"How could you be so stupid?"

"I think you're a troll here!"

The fatal blow was an outcry from a woman who wrote, "You're no longer childfree by choice. Get the hell out of this site you fucking asshole! You're not welcomed here!"

I was appalled at the openly hateful stance that some people expressed. "Not to empathize with one of our own in a terrible predicament shocks me," I answered. "I'm against this volcanic dysentery some are spewing. I wonder how the people casting those verbal stones would feel in the same situation?" The reply stunned me. I was personally attacked in seething retribution.

I had encountered this woman before on another childfree support site. I looked at her personal Facebook page to see if she was an angry mom, as we sometimes encountered. There were no photos of children or any other references to her being a mother. Her photo wasn't flattering. She seemed to have a permanent sneer on her face, was in her forties, and used a lot of vulgarity in her comments. She continued with her verbal Molotov cocktail: "Childfree people are people who do *not* want children. They actively stay away from having kids, adopting kids, or raising kids. They don't have kids in their homes. They're not responsible for younger humans at all. Your group is made up of too many childless people, stepparents, and unhappy parents. You and your group are not childfree! You should have your lifetime achievement award taken back! You're a sham, a disgrace. You've blatantly revealed you're a stepmother in your memoir. You can't be childfree by choice! Nobody should read your book. Nobody should go on your childfree group cruises. Nobody should look to you for guidance."

My fingertips felt tingly. My heart raced. My stomach felt as if someone had punched it hard. I read and reread the ugly words, hoping to see them morph into something less jarring, less vindictive, and less alarming.

It took me back to the years when I faced death threats after appearing on *60 Minutes* and announcing I never wanted to be a parent. I saw the picket lines with signs reading "Godless Bitch" when I spoke at high schools on Long Island. I felt the same bewilderment that once permeated my body while police carefully escorted me past faces filled with rage. Those people believed I was about to poison the minds of their children against parenting when in fact I was trying to stem the tide of teenage pregnancies. I tried to dispel the myths and fluff with the hard realities of what parenting's responsibilities and costs really were. The utter frustration of being falsely accused of being a child hater left me dumfounded. I felt overcome, again.

It showed me that even amongst so-called like-minded people, hate reigns supreme if my definition of childfree is better than yours. Through the skewed perceptions of angry childfree people, I was being demonized and placed on the defensive. This was happening on a childfree Facebook page! The hatred and accusations came from people who claimed to be childfree by choice. How could this be happening?

Why would it matter if the word "childfree" meant different things to different people? Why would a revenge mentality take hold, insisting that one definition was better than another? How could anyone find joy in ridiculing, detesting, and slandering someone who faced a shocking, life-altering experience, like that now-pregnant woman? Why would I, who spent a lifetime trying to make the childfree lifestyle a viable, respected choice, even if I once held the title of stepparent, be reviled?

Perhaps the best answer I got was from a follower named Sarah:

"I believe some people get upset and feel the need to differentiate because those who decide *not* to have children get a very different reaction than those who wanted to but couldn't. There seems to be a bit more empathy for those unable to have children. Just my experience..."

Maybe she was right. There's more empathy toward those who face infertility, or try to be good stepparents. Parents who've embraced the childfree movement out of desperation, sadness, or total frustration with their hateful, vengeful children are given more empathy. Society still feels they *tried* to be parents. Being a parent in any way, shape, or form is usually a supreme title. The exceptions are parents who are known child abusers, drug addicts, or alcoholics. There's no love lost toward the too many parents who keep on procreating without regard for the issue of overpopulation.

Maybe these angry people within our ranks are so harassed, so confronted in their own family or work, that they can't stand the thought of any person with even a hint of connection to a child pretending to the title of childfree by choice? They protest too much because they hurt the most.

Some may be shunned by families that don't invite them to family events simply because they blatantly don't want kids. Some may face the loss of their job to people who are parents. Some may suffer from the constant accusations that they are selfish, immature, or doomed to regret their choice after it's too late to change. These attacks can cause irreparable damage to one's feeling of safety and self-respect.

Apparently, it's a touchy subject among many childfree people. Purists insist the only truly childfree-by-choice people have absolutely no connections whatsoever with children. They scoff at parents of estranged kids, the infertile, or even those who choose a profession around the needs of children. They can't be childfree by choice! Not now. Not ever, if they once accepted children into their lives. When Jim, my husband, heard this, he quipped, "Well, if I was a meat eater and was told it was bad for my health so I chose being a vegetarian, would I still be considered a meat eater?" That made me smile.

In my own definition, a childfree-by-choice person is someone who never wants to give birth or adopt children. They don't see the parenting lifestyle as one they wish to live, for many reasons. Some are faced with debilitating illnesses or mental challenges they don't want to replicate. Some are adamantly angry about the population explosion and feel a fierce need to not add to it. Some have a fear of pregnancy and birthing. Some have an aversion to children. However, there are some people who face infertility, spend years trying to conceive through IVF or other means, and finally accept that they won't be parents. Instead of viewing their life as "less," they choose to be childfree. They're no longer childless and facing the pity of others. They're free to live their lives any way they want without the societal burden of being barren.

There are childfree-by-choice stepparents who struggle with children born of other relationships. They didn't set out to fall in love with a partner who had kids, but they did. Although they do their best in a very difficult and demanding situation, they themselves would never choose to have a child. They tell their stepchildren, "I'm not your mother or father. I'm a friend."

There are also parents of estranged children whose ongoing abuse at the hands of those children led them to let go of their toxic offspring and become childfree by choice. Yes, they were once parents. But now, there is no connection with those children, who flicked them out of their lives like a dried booger. These are all childfree-by-choice people, in my opinion.

I have no objection to anyone's definition. It's an opinion. Everyone is entitled to them. However, when people are attacked for their difference of opinion with vitriol, abusive language, and hostility, I recoil. Just because I didn't fit another person's definition, I was attacked and deemed unworthy, when in fact I've been a pioneer and passionate leader in this movement. The people attacking me never met or spoke with me! Their stories were created for their own needs. The angry woman I mentioned earlier took a passage from my first book out of context, making it sound like I once wanted to have children. She neglected to include other paragraphs within that book describing why I felt that way, and how pronatalism affected those momentary uncertainties, which, I want to make clear, are shared by many people.

All this drama and rejection from within led me to think about the various definitions of childfree by choice. Here's a chart I came up with. I fall into the "Liberal" category. Where are you, dear reader?

Group	Description
Purists	• They never want to be near, have, raise, or adopt kids. • No childless or barren people are childfree. • No estranged parents, or stepparents, are childfree. • No people who choose to work with kids are childfree. • No person who allows kids into their home is childfree. • No person who enjoys their nieces or nephews or neighbors' kids is childfree. • If children move in next door, they'll consider moving. • If children come to the door selling candy or magazines, they will slam the door on them. • No kids are welcome on Halloween. (Purists may try to scare them by dressing like a witch or devil and screaming.)
Moderate	• They don't want to have, raise, or adopt children. • They may choose professions that help children, but aren't devoted to them. They'll do what's expected to the best of their ability, but nothing more. • They'll allow children in their home as long as a parent is with them.

- However, they refuse to child-proof that home, and warn parents to be mindful of their kids.
- They'll ask if a restaurant has a child-free area. If there's a screaming child, they'll ask to be moved.
- They may give out candy on Halloween. Chances are they'll go out for dinner that night and leave the house in darkness.
- They enjoy their nieces or nephews, but at a distance.
- They may have a pet.
- They'll send a gift to a favorite person or family choosing to have babies, but won't attend any baby shower.
- They'll leave money in their will for kids who are close to them. However, they plan to use as much of their money as they can before their deaths.
- If kids get too loud next door, they'll put on a record of "Yodeling to the Classics" and aim it outdoors toward the kids and grab a drink and some chocolate while giggling, since they aren't faced with the challenges of raising kids.
- They'll consider Disney as a vacation destination.
- They'll attend family events with kids, but will have a prepared excuse to

	leave just in case the kids or the pro-natalistic bullshit gets too annoying.
Liberal	<ul><li>They don't want to have, raise, or adopt children.</li><li>They will accept infertile people who now embrace child-freedom as being childfree by choice.</li><li>They'll accept stepparents as childfree by choice.</li><li>They'll accept estranged parents, and feel compassion for how awful those parents feel knowing their kids have thrown them out of their lives.</li><li>They may choose professions in which they interact with children and enjoy much of what they do with kids. They can be passionate teachers, doctors, or social workers.</li><li>They're devoted aunts and uncles, and will provide for their child relatives in their wills.</li><li>They may even leave money for favorite kids of close friends!</li><li>They may enjoy their neighbors' kids.</li><li>They enjoy Halloween, decorate their homes, and treat kids with candy that night.</li><li>They have a pet, or several pets, and call them "fur kids."</li><li>They'll go to baby showers and even take part in the silly games. However, they'll snicker to themselves, know-</li></ul>

ing they would never want this in their lives.

- If a family with children moves in next door, they may welcome them, but will secretly feel happy they don't have to put up with the endless demands of parenting.
- They look forward to family events with kids and may even take part in a game of hide-and-seek with them.
- Children are allowed in their homes. They may even offer to babysit knowing the kids will go back to their parents and they can return to their childfree lifestyle.
- They love Disney. The kids there don't bother them at all.

After I wrote this chart, I thought about how often we're defined by our differences, not the similarities we enjoy. Think about religion, politics, pro-life versus a woman's right to choose. I'm a secular humanist, but I see the joy that religion brings to some people, and I would never fault people who are religious. In politics we have a two-party system. Of course, there are differences! However, we all want our rights protected and this planet kept from harm. Regarding pro-life versus a woman's right to choose, neither side can feel the other's heartfelt feelings. Why can't both sides allow for differences rather than condemn? Can we ever reach out and say "we" or enjoy the infinite possibilities of "us" and the many issues on which we agree rather than disagree? In other words, why can't we find the common threads that attach our hearts: compassion, peace, good health, friends, and family?

That thought led me to make a list of the things I feel we agree upon within the childfree-by-choice movement. It doesn't matter if the childfree are purists, moderate, or liberal in their definition of childfree by choice. These are my ten common threads:

1. Pronatalism exists and must be stopped.

2. Childfree people are often shunned, maligned, and made to feel inferior, selfish, and immature.

3. The title of parent is revered.

4. There are no effective courses or classes that show the reality of raising children. There should be.

5. Myths about having or raising children abound. Not all children are precious and worth all the sacrifice.

6. Overpopulation is a real issue on this planet.

7. People without children can live full, happy lives without feeling alone or sad, or regretting their lifestyle choice at the end of their lives.

9. Raising children is expensive!

10. Not everyone is parent material.

I like reading these similarities. Unlike the differences in the table of childfree definitions, it makes me smile. It's like an oasis in the hostile desert of difference.

After the shock of betrayal and rejection from within, I went back to taking care of my Facebook pages even more determined to avoid people who can't accept me the way I am. I adore the positive remarks about how these Facebook pages, Instagram, Twitter, my books, and our childfree group cruises make a difference in so many lives.

Rejection from within will continue. I simply accept

the fact. Differences of opinions will continue. It's human nature. Instead of fighting back like a Malcolm X, I'll embrace the Gandhi or Martin Luther King mentality. However, I won't buy in to the bullying and ignorance that differences of opinion can generate. No matter what category you fall into—purist, moderate, or liberal—we all agree that the childfree lifestyle is a viable choice. As a movement, we need to stand united, not divided, and be determined to define our lifestyle as a respected and viable alternative to parenting.

Chapter 11
Rejection:
A Tale of Acceptance, by Sam Nugent

Introduction from Marcia:

When one of my Facebook followers requested information about our first group cruise, I couldn't believe what I learned. She was from Australia! Would she really want to travel to Miami, Florida, just to be with us? The length of that flight would have me sucking my thumb in a fetal position. Her reply was simple and haunting: "I need to see *you* in person! Emailing, texting, or even Skyping won't do. I finished reading your memoir. It's more than a casual read. It's life-changing. I'm not the person I was before reading your book. I have things I must share in person."

It wasn't until I made the reservation for her, received her deposit, and then final payment that I believed she would actually make the long trip!

On the day of our cruise, I was excited. There were many people coming with us. I wanted them to have a terrific time and make happy memories. I especially looked forward to meeting Samantha. I was determined to find her in the preboarding area before boarding that ship. She was alone! She had just traveled more than twenty-four hours! "How will I know you?" I'd emailed her before she left. She answered, "My flaming short red hair! Besides, I'll know you from your photo on your book. I'll find you!"

And she did!

I didn't know what our week together would mean to her, or to me. What she shared and how profoundly it affected me still makes me tear up. She illuminated the physical need to meet people who don't want to have children in person. I also learned that there are still places where you may think you're the only person on the planet who doesn't want children! Hearing about like-minded people or reading about them isn't the same as being with them. Having met Samantha, and having written about rejection internationally in Chapter 9, it's clear to me child-freedom still isn't a widely known or respected lifestyle choice in some parts of the world.

The lesson I took from meeting Samantha and learning her story, which follows, is to continue touching people's lives in positive ways by overcoming pronatalism. If that means writing more books, I'll do it. If it means more opportunities to meet at events, I'll support it.

Talk about having a life purpose!

Three years have gone by since we met. Since then, Samantha and I have Skyped, Zoomed, emailed, and even spoken by phone (when we could get the hours straight) to stay connected. When she heard I was writing a second book, she was excited. Toward the end of writing this book, I had an idea. I wanted you to hear her story. There's so much to be learned from her metamorphosis from a fearful woman victimized by rejection to a force to be reckoned with in her private life and in the childfree lifestyle. I asked her to write her story for you. She agreed. Here it is:

As far back as I can remember, raising children was never one of my life goals. Child-freedom wasn't even a word in my lexicon. When the thought of not wanting kids flickered in my brain, I pushed it aside. Then, I made excuses such as, "My dysfunctional childhood is the reason I don't want children." It seemed a good excuse.

I've come to learn that a dysfunctional childhood is an experience that's common among people who don't want to have or raise children. However, it's an experience that not all childfree people share. Many come from wonderful childhood experiences. The choice to live a childfree lifestyle, and the experience of rejection, often seems to come later, whether you've suffered a terrible childhood or experienced a supportive, loving one. However, good or bad childhoods didn't matter to me, because in 2015 I'd never met a childfree-by-choice person, and I wasn't sure they existed!

The experience of many children that seemed to share my dysfunctional family background was to find a serviceable currency that helped them make friends. For some it was being the class clown, the raw intellect, the entertainer, or the bully. For me it was being the counselor.

From the earliest age I can recall, the only way I could connect with others and get them to spend time with me was by solving problems and giving them advice or being a shoulder to cry on. No issue was too big or too small. You would think that this would result in me having loads of friends, but you'd be wrong. What evolved was that I became a satellite orbiting the tight-knit cliques and galaxies of friends, a presence that was noted, but not embraced. A useful presence if anyone wanted to complain about other members of the established group without the core members finding out. Once the transaction of advice was completed, I'd be lucky to be acknowledged with more than a hello the following day. Most of my cohorts had the far more important task of getting back to their established group. Although there was no written rule, the terms of the transactions were very clear: time spent with me was in exchange for counseling received. Support or friendship would not be reciprocated under any circumstances. So it continued, me as the satellite, always available to any or all group members who needed me, alone when no one needed me.

Secrets were kept, transactions made. Business was good, but friendship was something that remained a mystery to me, and perhaps something I just wasn't worthy of.

In late high school and university, it was easier to make connections with men, until it became apparent what they were after! Still, by then I had given up on the prospect of ever having real friends like I saw on TV and dreamed of having. I realized the best I could hope for was pleasant interactions with "acquaintances," some of whom still required a payment of counseling services for their time. I longed for adventures, friends, and love. I also had a thirst for traveling. In my dreams, I would travel with friends.

I traveled alone. Unlike most of my acquaintances in Australia, my traveling reveries never included children, or returning from my trips into the open arms of waiting children. You may think wanting a child would make me feel there was a possibility of profound love to overcome the chasm of feeling alone. Not at all!

Some acquaintances had mentioned as early as high school their goal of "settling down and having children." Many were clear on how many children they wanted, and even names, but the idea was completely foreign to me. At the time, these people who were so ardent about the idea of family had come from good families. I'd met their seemingly perfect parents and siblings. It seemed this was an obvious prerequisite for wanting children. It reinforced my belief that because I hadn't come from such a family, I was incapable of seeing their perspective.

The drive to secure independence through an income was a strong motivator in my early adulthood. I felt that if I had money, then I could explore more social opportunities and maybe I'd find friends. I couldn't pursue my adventurous dream of becoming an archaeologist or anthropologist, or studying world cultures and ancient histories and beliefs, because it would take too long. My parents also indirectly but frequently reminded me that I couldn't make money that way. The many passions and interests I had in the arts were not quick pathways to income, so I fell back into what I knew I was good at, which at least gave me some satisfaction from helping people: counseling.

It was easy to excel in the area. After all, while most of my cohorts could only rely on their experience and studies from university, I'd been working as a psychologist and counselor since I was seven years old! So, by the time I was actually getting paid in money instead of human company for my skills, I had well over ten years of experience.

The transition from studies into working life was an easy one. I didn't mourn the loss of contact with close friends in high school because I didn't have any to lose! I had a respected skill that I could use to help others, and I was lauded for being extremely good at it, and was both liked and respected by the acquaintances (now colleagues) that I worked with, who wondered how on earth I got so good at counseling so young. Surely, I'd now finally make friends! Well, no! You would think, again, that having a child would be the thought to make me feel I could have an endless, loving, caring heart connection. Not once did this thought come into my brain. Child-freedom was still more appealing.

The group of working adults was now a different population from the cohorts of children, teenagers, and young adults I was used to in university. This group was clearer about what they wanted out of life. They didn't seem like a group that considered a variety of different lifestyles, or viewed the world as full of choice and possibilities. If they were younger, they were out to have a good time with friends and find a life partner in the next few years before they settled down to marry and have kids. If they were older, it was family, home, and career stability to provide for the children. There was a diversity of ages, but one thing was clear: having children was a definite eventuality in adulthood. Not one person talked about the possibility of living a life without the responsibilities of raising children. Child-freedom was verboten.

The people who surrounded me at work, be they colleagues or clients, were all adamant. It was the "done thing" at some stage, most likely between twenty and thirty. You'll get married and have children. It was normal.

Time passed, my career progressed. Relationships with both male and female colleagues took on more of a social form. I was part of teams, many of which worked collaboratively, or did similar work to mine. There was more to talk about than just providing counsel to colleagues. People seemed to like me for who I was. I felt a step closer to making friends for the first time in my life.

Then, the inevitable question arose. I met a man, thought I was in love, and married him. After my co-workers knew we'd married, I heard, "When are you going to have children?" Neither of us ever talked about children! Not sure why! Initially, I honestly replied to the questions, "I don't want children." I soon learned this was a big mistake. Honesty was *not* the best policy. What I had inadvertently done was blown my best chance to have real friends. My admission to colleagues that I didn't want children was met with an audible gasp of shock. "But you'd be such a good mother!" they replied, aghast, clearly having no insight into my own upbringing or belief in my own maternal skills. "Maybe," I replied, foolishly going on. "I just have never had the urge, or felt I would be." Then their expression of shock changed to one of pity. "You're still young, you'll change your mind," these mothers said, almost as if to reassure me, like I was errant in my immaturity, and the "light" that would illuminate the righteous and correct path of motherhood had not yet switched on.

We then got back to work. I thought the mothering conversation was over. It was over, but not in the way I thought, which was that we would all move on as normal colleagues in a workplace. Their attitude toward me changed. I clearly recalled memories of school days, where if I sat down at lunch with a group, everyone would stop talking or look for a reason to move away. I had no place there unless someone wanted me for counseling. Conversations with me were limited to only work. Invitations to join in other social gatherings ceased. Rejection reared its ugly head again.

As my career evolved and I progressed into new teams

and job roles, I started grasping what was clearly separating me from the others. Someone would announce a pregnancy, or worse yet bring a baby into the office, where shrieks of delight from the women echoed admiration and support. I couldn't understand why they all ran to dote on and gush over the baby. It wasn't like someone brought a dog or cat into the office, or a cake! I just didn't get the appeal. In fact, it annoyed me. Not only did it interrupt my workday, but it also made me acutely aware of just how isolated and different I was from my colleagues. I felt like a freak, rejected for not feeling the same way as other women about babies. Maybe something was wrong with me? Each time someone recognized me as a "woman of a certain age," I was bluntly asked, "So? When are you having children?" I'd learned my lesson. Honesty was now off the table. I had to find better responses, such as, "Oh, not for a while yet!" This was delivered with a cheeky smile, or an added, "I'm still too young to have children," which was always responded to with a reassuring, "Oh, your time will come," or some other response that confirmed the imminence and unavoidable nature of having a baby.

As I got into my late twenties and then thirties, the responses grew bolder in their expression of pity and prying into why I didn't have a child yet. Intrusively suspicious assumptions prevailed: there must be some medical reason I was unable to have children. No objective reason I gave for not having a child—not age, finances, or life stability—was sufficient for those interrogating me.

I adapted to these work teams, accepting the reality again that I would never have friends and would just be an outcast who never had children. The accepted word for my condition, from their perspective, was "workaholic" or "career woman." Sometimes new women who hadn't yet had children would join the team and I would get my hopes up. I never asked them if they wanted children, or when they were going to have them. I figured that would be an appreciated and welcome change. We could talk, and did, about work, travel, hobbies, relationships, TV, the arts, anything and everything! Maybe I had finally found a friend!

Each time, the inevitable happened. They became pregnant, and for some reason that to this day I don't understand, their ability or willingness to talk about anything other than children instantly went away, seemingly replaced by their rejection of me, making me the outcast again. Worse yet, I was perceived as a lying outcast who again had to continually dodge the topic of why I was rejecting the joy of having children. The colleague I had mistakenly thought was a friend now had far more important and illustrious circles to move in. Motherhood circles. Circles where women always have something to share and talk about: their children! It was never-ceasing. Everything was about children, as if there was nothing else of importance or relevance in their lives, or mine.

This soon evolved into a clear expectation that I not take, and not be approved for, leave near long weekends or school holidays, and that I work late to cover colleagues "because I don't have children." Compared to the pedestal-dwelling mothers, I felt like a second-class citizen, less than a woman, and a freak because I had no children. Any requests to management or HR for leave at times that just happened to be school holidays were consistently rejected.

I was also saddled with the responsibility to complete projects or "just suck it up" and modify my entire schedule to cover for colleagues who had sick children, because "you don't have kids at home." It didn't seem to matter that other colleagues could have shared the work to cover for the mother with a sick child! Their schedules weren't in any way negotiable, and "took priority" because they had to get home for their own kids.

The message was clear: my life and my time weren't as important in the workplace as my colleagues who were mothers. I wasn't as important or valued. I made the mistake of pushing back, calling it discriminatory to consider my time less important. Although it frightened me to state my truths, there was also a feeling of conquest. Didn't I have the right to my own opinions? Wasn't this a flagrant act of discrimination against non-parents? That just seemed to open the floodgates of their real feelings toward me. "You must hate children," one person said when I slipped up and told a group of colleagues I didn't want children. Another, thinking I was out of earshot, said, "She's one of those monsters that don't want children." Giggles ensued from other group members. "Weirdo," they snickered amongst themselves. They occasionally glanced back toward me with a blend of anger, pity, and resentment. I heard, "How can anyone not want children?"

About this time, my first marriage ended. It wasn't right for either of us and had nothing to do with not having children. My path changed dramatically from being married and working in a corporate setting. I resolved to never work for someone else again. I could be self-employed, so I would be. I was peaceful in my isolation and in getting to know myself without a man. No one brought babies to my office. No questions about when I was going to have children. Some much-needed space between me and mother talk.

By this time, the Internet had come into being. I started searching for other people's stories about not wanting children. At the time, there really wasn't much. Most sites I found seemed to chronicle the stories of people who desperately wanted children but could not conceive them, or they were support groups for infertility. Then, suddenly, a book stood out. That book was *Confessions of a Childfree Woman*, by Marcia Drut-Davis. I ordered it immediately.

In a couple of weeks, the book arrived. To say I couldn't put it down is an understatement. I read it cover to cover in a day and then again, multiple times over the coming weeks. I almost had to be reassured the words I'd read before were still there the way I originally read them! I'd finally found someone in the world like me, who thought like me and seemed to share many of the same values. Although, unlike me, she had a terrific childhood (until her parents divorced, leaving her feeling like an outcast in the new family of her mom, stepfather, and newborn sister), she didn't want children. For the first time in my life I felt that maybe, just maybe, I wasn't alone. This woman had lived longer than I had. She not only survived, but was capable of having long-term friends and successful relationships. Some were even parents! Her story gave me hope I had never thought possible for someone like me.

We both shared in the rejection of our childfree choice. However, she was able to come out the other side and not just survive, but thrive. Even losing her job after exposure on *60 Minutes* and facing irate parents picketing when she spoke didn't stop her. So I reached out to Marcia. I had no expectations, because she was an American author. I was just some random person from Australia. I wanted to thank her for sharing her story. I needed to tell her how her memoir allowed me to feel like I was no longer alone in my experience.

I was shocked when Marcia wrote back! That started a correspondence between us where we could share our experiences. For the first time in my life I felt like someone actually wanted to learn about who I was as a person, and would listen to me without expecting counseling or asking for something in return. To feel accepted by someone was a completely new experience.

Born and raised in Australia, I always wanted to go to the United States and the Caribbean. But cruising and sightseeing wasn't the real pull. My main purpose was to meet the woman who changed my life. Before reading her book, I had never known anyone who never wanted children. I'd always tried to blame my lack of desire to have children on my challenging upbringing, rather than simply seeing child-freedom as a viable, normal lifestyle. After reading the last words on the last page of her book, I felt a weight lift off my heart. I was fine just the way I was. Not only that, but according to what Marcia shared, it was a fabulous lifestyle that offered the freedom to do what I want and pursue my dreams wherever they take me.

Of course, it would be an added perk to meet other like-minded people! However, I was nervous. What if Marcia didn't like me? What if I couldn't relate to the other childfree people on the cruise, or fit in with anyone? I was scared by past rejections, and negative thoughts lingered.

What I gained from the cruise was more balance and perspective than I could have ever hoped for. The balance came from the realization that not only were there more people like me, but they had such varied backgrounds! I learned that not everyone came from dysfunction. They had all sorts of different reasons for choosing not to have children. I learned that while I got on well with everyone, that didn't mean we'd all become forever friends. But several of us did! They were capable of liking me for who I am, not just for what they could get from me. Most importantly, I saw something in Marcia that I had never seen in anyone else before. Marcia was Marcia. No agenda, no judgment, just a person capable of accepting me fully for who I am and wanting nothing in return.

Finally, for the first time in my life, I had a friend.

My world then opened up in new ways I could never have imagined. My life changed for the better. The possibility of friends and the validity of a childfree lifestyle helped fuel my then-new relationship, which eventually became my second marriage, which almost ten years later is flourishing. My own definitions and expectations of friendship changed for the better, opening me up to new friendships and more types and depths of friendship than I could have ever imagined. Just by not feeling alone, my ability to relate to other people, including mothers, dramatically improved. I no longer feared rejection by them. Even though there is still rejection, it no longer comes from the only people in my world! Sometimes it only takes that one special person who, just by being themselves, empowers others with the bravery and acceptance to just be *them*selves. And for me, that was Marcia.

I share this because if my story reaches one person, as Marcia reached me with her memoir, and her acceptance of me, it might change their life forever. Having a heart connection reciprocated is a feeling I never had until I met her, in person, on that cruise. Now I have it with my beloved second husband. Since meeting Marcia I've totally changed my career goals. I'm now starting a business to support childfree people facing rejection. I also want to counsel and support unhappy parents, if they're brave enough to admit it. Too many parents, sadly, are disillusioned about parenting, or have estranged children. I want to help them see how they can overcome the shock of pronatalism's broken promises.

I didn't have the understanding or the tools to recognize the rejection I'd faced until I read Marcia's memoir and met her in person. I blamed myself and never knew how to overcome it. I thought I was the reason I had no friends, when, perhaps, those who rejected me were the real reasons. I've now come to see that there are others in Australia and all over the world who need to read my story. I'm a happy, proud, and fulfilled childfree woman.

Chapter 12
Rejecting Cancer

"I long to believe in immortality."
—John Keats, letter to Fanny Brawne (1818)

Dr. Roberts looked upset. After asking me to get dressed and meet him in his office, he walked out mumbling, "I'm very concerned. Don't like what I see."

I didn't want to see him in his damned office, so I dressed in slow motion. The word "concerned" vibrated long after the sound of his clicking footsteps disappeared down the hall.

My own concern over my symptoms was mounting. Although another gastroenterologist had said it was "just a hemorrhoid," the pain, bleeding, and feeling of malaise mounted. I liked that doctor; I'd gone to him for fourteen years. He was considered one of the best gastro-enterologists in the area. I wanted to believe him! But.

People who say "Listen to your body and inner wisdom" have it right. Had I not done that, I don't think you'd be reading this.

I finished dressing, opened the door, and found Dr. Roberts' assistant waiting to escort me into the dreaded office. I was surprised to see Jim, looking frightened and somber, already sitting in front of the doctor's desk. He'd wanted to accompany me on this appointment because he feared the results, especially after hearing me complain more and more about the increasing bleeding and pain. I relented, though I asked him to stay in the outside waiting room and watch TV during my examination.

I have a friend whose husband stays with her during

medical exams. I didn't want that. One person peering into my anus was enough.

Jim looked upset, as if he were about to vomit. The color had drained from his sweet face. Had Dr. Roberts mumbled "I'm very concerned" to Jim, too?

I slowly sat down, feeling weak. "Well, I can see this isn't good news."

Dr. Roberts wasted no time. "You have anal cancer," he blurted out. "I need to do a colonoscopy to be sure. I'll take a small amount of tissue, then examine further into your rectum and colon to be sure nothing else looks suspicious. The biopsy will confirm my fears." He was intensely blunt and overtly uncaring, devoid of compassion. Heartless, even.

I'd rarely felt so much hate as I did in that moment. *How can he be so sure without a biopsy?* I thought. Then I got the courage to actually say that.

He shuffled some papers on his desk and, without looking up, said, "Because I'm good at what I do. Wish I could tell you it's going to be fine. It isn't. You're in for a tough time. You're going to need two weeks of twenty-four-hour-a-day chemo, with additional radiation treatments for about thirty-eight days. You'll have open, painful burns and sores from your rectum to your vagina from the radiation. When you urinate or defecate, it will burn like hell cascading over those open wounds. You'll probably lose your hair from the chemo, too."

My eyes met Jim's and I fought back tears.

I had read all about such medical dramas from friends or family in emails, texts, and on Facebook. Though anyone can get cancer at any time, the stories I heard always seemed to be a direct result of aging. From time to time, people would call me to reveal the newest cancer statistic or, sadly, its most recent victim. Lunch dates would leave me feeling sickened as friends shared awful news about so-and-so facing the ravages of chemo or radiation. I would think, *Awful. Terrible. Glad it's not me!* I wondered if they'd soon be thinking the same about me.

Seeing that I was about to lose it, Dr. Roberts managed to drum up some understanding and a hint of compassion. He actually sat forward as if to reach out to me, then dug deep into his cold, tin-man heart.

"This isn't going to be a walk in the park," he said more softly. "I won't sugarcoat anything; it's not my style. But I'm good at what I do. I'll pinpoint this so you can start treatment immediately. The sooner, the better."

I found myself saying, "If you're so sure it's cancer, why have a biopsy?" I'd totally forgotten he'd already answered that question. My brain felt like Jell-O.

"Because without that proven diagnosis, you won't find any doctor who'll treat it," he flatly replied, then continued with a slight sneer: "Your other doctor said it was a bleeding hemorrhoid, remember? Proof is a must before any cancer treatment."

Jim finally spoke up. "What's the prognosis?"

"Not sure until we know what stage she's in or if any lymph nodes are involved," Dr. Roberts said. "The biopsy will answer that. If it's Stage I without any lymph nodes involved, there's an 80 percent possibility she'll beat this and live a long life."

My first thread of hope. But then my next thought came: *What if I'm in the other 20 percent?* Isn't it funny how delicious hope can turn to fear and pessimism in a flash? Instead of focusing on the 80 percent possibility that

I would live a long life, I became fixated on the 20 percent chance of an agonizing, untimely death.

Changing negative thoughts to positive ones has always been a theme in my speeches and lectures about the childfree lifestyle. Statistics proved that people are happier without raising kids. The realities of child-rearing are apparent: It's not always wonderful! It's very expensive! It's a twenty-four-hour-a-day, seven-day-a-week job!

Now I'd have to listen to my own advice and learn to choose positive thoughts when dealing with this health challenge. It wasn't easy.

Positive thought: Treatment will stop this.

Negative thought: Not necessarily!

Positive thought: Of course it will.

Negative thought: But 20 percent die!

Positive thought: But we found it in time.

Negative thought: But maybe we didn't!

"Why did my body betray me?" I screamed on the drive home. Didn't I eat the right whole foods and stay away from sugar and dairy? Didn't I exercise and do yoga? Hadn't I experienced less stress because of my childfree lifestyle? Research shows that being childfree brings less stress than the incessant demands of raising kids. Stress is believed to be a major cause of many illnesses. So what gives?

Of course, Dr. Roberts was right, and it was soon confirmed: I had anal cancer, Stage I with no affected lymph nodes. I was in the 80 percent, with a fighting chance of beating the cancer. That became my mantra.

I suddenly had hope and determination. Losing to the disease wasn't an option. Fear tried to knock me out, over and over, but I tried to choose positive thoughts. If cancer was going to punch me, I was going to punch right back.

I faced the treatments with the vengeance of a warrior. It wasn't going to get me. I wasn't going to be among the 20 percent.

And so I started on a path I'd never taken before: a journey to save my life. My body had rejected me in a mean, vengeful way. It was a different type of rejection than I'd suffered after proclaiming on national TV that I never wanted to have kids. That rejection led to a lost job. The rejection I now faced could lead to the loss of my life.

The next two weeks were a blur of blood tests and assembling my medical team. Once that was in place, I underwent a procedure to place a port on the upper-right side of my chest, for easier administration of chemo. Since it would be a two-week, twenty-four-hour-a-day treatment, I'd have to wear a shoulder-bag-like apparatus containing the toxic concoction, which was called fluorouracil, or 5-FU. *FU?* You can't make this stuff up.

The day they set me up with the take-home chemo, something happened that I never expected to experience as a happy childfree woman. It had nothing to do with any of the treatments. As I was taken into a large room that smelled of medicinal concoctions, I observed several people sitting in lounge chairs. Some were reclined and sleeping; others watched TV. Some looked very, very sick, blanket-wrapped and with yellowed complexions. Some had no hair, some wore obvious wigs, and some women had adorned themselves with scarves cleverly knotted to hide their balding heads. A few were staring through large windows into the garden outside. Others chatted with the nurses who were administering to their needs. Ominous bottles, hung from poles, were attached to people's veins. Some had only one bottle. Others had many. I wondered how many I would have attached to my port.

Kaiko, my nurse, showed me the three bottles labeled as mine. One was an anti-nausea medication. The other two were the evil potions intended to kill my cancer. I snickered when I saw the 5-FU name she placed in front of me. I would be taking them home for an entire week, after several hours of supervision that first day in the treatment center. (This process would then repeat four weeks later.) They wanted to observe me for any bad reactions. Once the chemo slowly began to drip through the tubes and into my body, they tipped the lounge chair back and I rested. Jim stayed next to me as my cheerleader and loving support, ready to flag down Kaiko at a moment's notice.

As I lay there, I observed the people sitting next to my fellow patients: mates, lovers, partners, relatives, co-workers, friends, neighbors.

Two were alone, and that made me sad. I couldn't imagine being alone when such an illness struck. Although who's to say these two wanted anyone next to them? Maybe they had their own versions of Jim but asked him or her to stay home so they could do this alone.

Other patients were watched over by their children. One woman introduced her daughter to me. Another man introduced his two sons.

I was caught off guard by the quick pang of regret. Although I was glad to have Jim there, we had no child to take over the next shift. No offspring to pass along my DNA. My bare branch on the family tree was about to snap off with a final and thunderous *crack*, and there would be nobody there to carry me into immortality.

As a childfree woman, I had never felt remorse about not producing a child, and couldn't care less about what happened after my death... until I was staring it in the face. *Had I made a mistake?* This thought shocked me, especially after I'd written an entire book about the joys of not having children. Was this an authentic regret, or was the cultural brainwashing finally catching up to me?

I looked down at my crooked fingers and saw my mom's hands. I caught my reflection in the mirror and saw my father's eyes staring back at me.

I hadn't passed down my mother's hands and my father's eyes. They would die with me. This cancer would carry us all into oblivion.

Slowly I managed to push away these thoughts and choose more rational thinking. Yes, the children sitting next to these patients carried many of their parents' physical attributes. Including, most likely, a genetic predisposition to cancer and a distinct possibility that one day they'd be sitting in the same lounge chairs their parents now occupied.

I wondered about the connection between these children and parents. Was it one of love, happy memories, and compassion? Did these children fervently want their parents to beat cancer, and would they continue to fill their parents' lives with love and support? I hoped so.

But maybe these children were here only out of guilt for being inattentive when their parents were well. Maybe some were thinking only of the things they'd inherit. Maybe some were reflecting on the physical and/or emotional abuse these parents had heaped on them in childhood.

I know! That's a terrible thought. But the world is full of shocking, gut-wrenching stories of estrangement and ill-equipped parents and monster children. I thought about Jim's two daughters, who chose to divorce us without ever telling us why. When Jim went through radiation treatments for prostate cancer, they never visited or called.

I returned my attention to those patients undergoing chemo alone. Were they like me, childfree by choice, or childless by fate? Or, perhaps worse, did they have children who lived too far away, or from whom they were estranged? There is never any guarantee that children can or will be there when you need them.

My mind took me back to thoughts of mortality. When I died, what would I leave behind? Again, no DNA. But hadn't I helped shape the future through the students I had the pleasure of teaching? Many of them were still in my life. Hadn't I planted trees and bushes that would provide beauty and oxygen after I was gone? Hadn't I volunteered to help poor Mexican parents learn English so that they and their children could have better futures? And hadn't I been given the first lifetime achievement award by an international committee supporting International Childfree Day? Didn't that mean I'd helped many people learn to appreciate the joys of the childfree lifestyle? Hadn't I written a book that would inspire, support, and educate people long after I'm gone?

Immortality isn't that great if the only form it takes is DNA. Because let's face it: sometimes DNA isn't so wonderful.

I looked to my right and smiled at the loving man sitting next to me. I looked to my left and saw dedicated nurses, doctors, and other professionals ready to help me in any way necessary. I thought about the friends and neighbors who had volunteered to bring homemade soups or take me to treatments when Jim couldn't. My dog would welcome me home every day after the grueling radiation treatments, licking my face and telling me she cared.

With these thoughts, I finally relaxed. Did it really matter that I had no children, or that my branch of the family tree would end at my death?

What you do here and now, for yourself and for others, for animals and for non-sentient beings, matters a hell of a lot more than creating life only to ensure your immortality.

Although cancer wasn't a walk in the park, as any survivor knows, life would soon get even sweeter for me. A funny thing happens when a potentially fatal illness invades you: You really take notice of life! The clouds had never looked more beautiful. Rainbows took my breath away. My husband's love had never filled me with such wonder. My dog's antics had never been funnier or more precious.

My life became a musical. Rain on the windows was a symphony. The sandhill cranes returning to our preserve every night with their raucous *caw caw caw*, an opera. Wind in my ears was an orchestra. I put on daily concerts in the shower and recitals at the piano. How could I have been so deaf to all this music before?

Once I saw how my thoughts influenced my results, I understood what I had to do. I'm not saying it was easy. There were times I had to scream "STOP THINKING THAT WAY" before I could return to positive thoughts. I didn't allow pronatalism and cultural conditioning to cloud the way I view my life choices, and I didn't allow myself to fear mortality simply because I was childfree. Living here now is what's most important.

Once I understood that, rejection lost.

When I depart this life, I won't be thinking about the child I never had. Hopefully I won't have any regrets at all. At worst I may say, "Damn it, I wish I had taken those Latin dancing lessons!"

But not if I go call that dance studio right now. If you'll excuse me.

Chapter 13
Eliminating Rejection: Is it possible?

"The harder the conflict, the more glorious the triumph!"
—Thomas Paine

Across the wall of the classroom in which I taught English as a Second Language from 1990 to 2000 was a phrase written in large, bold letters: **Never Stop Trying**.

For my international students arriving in a new country filled with foreign customs and foods and an even stranger language, that sign offered the encouragement they needed. Never stop! Never give in! Push your boundaries to get past the obstacle ahead of you, even if you already see another obstacle in front of that one. I would dramatically tell them, "You *will* find another wall in front of you!" And I'd continue with, "Stop whining 'Why me?' and instead say 'Why *not* me?'"

Over the years, many of my students told me that this one mantra got them through many of life's challenges. That simple phrase helps, too, in knowing how to face the inevitable rejection that comes with the childfree lifestyle. It also comes in handy when we try to bridge the gap between being rejected and rejecting others because of our differences of opinion. In other words, it helps stop the push-pull dance of "I'm right and you're wrong, damn it."

Truth be told, I hate the word "try" (even though I used it in the previous paragraph!). As Yoda of *Star Wars* wisely said, "Do or do not. There is no try." Think about it. Either you do something or you don't. How can you *try*? Yet I approach this chapter with a fervent hope that I can *try* (don't judge me) to get people to come together within this childfree/childless-versus-parenting conflict, despite all the rejection.

I've written about the pain of rejection suffered by childfree people whose families can't accept that choice. Until I interviewed people who revealed the truth, I never knew about the favoritism toward parents in our military. Internationally, I've heard from people who have been punished—often with frightening severity—by societies that lag years behind even our outdated American culture. The rejection I personally experienced from angry people within the childfree movement was my own rude awakening. To be called a sham and a fake because I once took the title of stepparent and had a "fur kid" exemplified the great divide between the purists, the moderates, and the liberal childfree. Then there are the childfree by fate, who face rejection by their own bodies. I never knew the grief that comes with trying to accept the word "childfree" versus "childless." How could I? I never tried to have a child!

At work, the childfree may feel rejection when parents are allowed to go home early, even though childfree people may have ailing parents or pets, or be suffering from a relentless migraine. "Too bad!" they're told. Nothing compares to the needs of a child.

Through my battle with cancer, I learned lessons about what immortality means (and doesn't mean) and who was there to help me when I most needed it. The fear that had been instilled in me about growing old and/or sick without a child to care for me dissipated.

Travel can be filled with its own brand of rejection. The shouting-down of our pleas for childfree areas on planes, in restaurants, and at hotels show how we face rejection for even thinking about our own needs. Think of how defensively a parent will act if we give even one look of annoyance when their kids are kicking our airplane seat.

Also all too common is the heartache of rejection and broken promises when one partner in a childfree relationship changes his or her mind. And a topic long ignored is now being discussed: men, too, face rejection for not wanting children. For too long it's been about only women. Clearly men have many challenges, too.

Ultimately, I've shown how to overcome rejection and protect the deep-rooted choice to remain childfree.

The burning question I've often asked myself is, *Can rejection of the childfree lifestyle ever be remedied?* Forty-five years after I "came out" on *60 Minutes* in 1974, I still get people asking me if I have any regrets. They seem to want to hear, "Of course I have regrets." That's not my truth. But when I tell them that, they seem disappointed.

My followers on Facebook and other websites supporting the childfree choice often vent about the topics I've covered in this book and in my memoir. I thought that after forty-five years there might be a shift toward acceptance of this personal choice. Was I wrong? I decided to post a question on Facebook:

"Question of the Day: Do you think there's a way we can ever bridge the gap resulting in rejection between parents and non-parents or childfree versus childless? How?"

There were nearly fifty responses the first day. Clearly the question hit a nerve. Here are a few of them:

Kristi: "I do think it will happen. Interracial

relationships were seen as taboo as little as twenty to thirty years ago, and now they're accepted by most. Then, people were against homosexuals and people who choose nontraditional romantic relationships. Now, gay marriage is legal and is accepted by a lot more people. I think the childfree bridge will be crossed in the near future, possibly in my lifetime. We already have childfree people speaking out about not regretting their choice. Now we just need more parents to admit their challenges raising children and, sadly, for some, remorse after having children!"

Many agreed with Kristi, sharing how their families now leave them alone and how people at work have stopped asking when they would have kids. Some mentioned that people at social gatherings and special events no longer dare to suggest that the childfree are selfish, irresponsible, or hedonistic.

Al: "I'm open and proud to say I don't want to have children. My parents totally support me. I've even heard them tell others to leave me alone if they hear some flak about my choice from other relatives."

LaQuisha: "My best friend has two kids. She keeps saying she totally supports my choice. Once she told me if I ever felt the need, she would gladly let me care for hers any time I wanted to! Then we both broke out laughing. It felt good because she gets me and I get her! We both feel comfortable sharing our truths."

Then there was this jarring answer to my question about whether we can ever bridge the gap between parents and non-parents:

Rhonny: "No!"

After reading that one-word comment, I stared at my keyboard for what seemed an eternity. Was Rhonny right?

Can we never bridge this chasm of rejection?

That "No!" led to writer's block. I kept reaching for that come-together moment, but it kept feeling further and further away. To a writer, nothing is more upsetting than not being able to write a single word. It's the kiss of death.

Rhonny's "No!" reverberated through me. I'm a Libra; I look for ways to balance the good with the bad. Could I find answers to overcoming rejection in the childfree lifestyle? Surely I could offer some concrete ideas to counter Rhonny's negativity.

From past writing blocks, I knew I needed to get away from my computer. After bending down to pet my dog, who was snoring, oblivious to my block, I stretched and went downstairs to the refrigerator to eat some salted-caramel ice cream.

I found it nestled in the back of the freezer. After slowly downing the delectable, cold ambrosia from the gods, I felt a renewed energy. (Although I also felt guilty because the ice cream was going straight to my hips and clogging my aging arteries with more cholesterol!) After I sat back down at the computer, the words came pouring out.

With this new book, I wanted to share the wisdom of an aging woman fighting for respect and acceptance while overcoming rejection of the childfree lifestyle. Having personally faced rejection, and having researched and interviewed many people about their own rejection, I wanted to give you a glimmer of optimism in this chapter. I didn't want to leave you feeling disheartened or depressed about all the rejection you've read about in this book. My vision was of a circle of parents and non-parents, the childfree and the childless, holding hands across the globe and singing "Kumbaya."

Rejection is among the most unwelcome feelings. I experience it when I'm made to feel less adequate by another's words or behaviors. It's abusive, a form of bullying. You know the feeling: it's one of helplessness, like you're a victim with no recourse. You can temporarily push these feelings away, but you'll find that they always return. Raw emotions such as vulnerability, victimization, defensiveness, anger, shock, and bewilderment may come in waves. Even if you manage to get the anger out through verbal retaliation, you still end up feeling rejected, perhaps even worse than before.

When rejection rears its ugly head, you feel like you must strike back or defend your personal beliefs. Your reactions may start out calm, but when you keep hearing these personal attacks you may feel your blood pressure rising.

I'm not suggesting you need to become adversarial. People have the right to their own beliefs, even if you feel they're ignorant and/or brainwashed.

I'm going to continue to speak up and share my thoughts and concerns about people who continue to procreate without regard for this planet. However, I won't stoop to their tactic of shaming us by saying we're the selfish ones for not wanting to raise children. I'll continue to ask questions in the hope that they'll rethink why they do what they do. I'll do this with dignity. I'll never threaten them, browbeat them, name-call them, or attack them for their choices. Why would I do that if I don't want it done to me?

To those who use the words "mombies" and "moos"

for mothers or "crotch-droppings" and "devil's spawns" for children, I can only say: what does that teach? It's the "I'm right and you're wrong" syndrome. Which leads to more irrational thinking, and lots of "I'll find an equally offensive thing to say to you."

Let's show some compassion to those facing infertility. Let's reach out to them and help them overcome their socio-pronatalistic brainwashing, which leads them to feel "barren" when in fact their lives can be full, productive, and joyful. Let's not insist they try another round of expensive in vitro procedures, find a surrogate, or adopt. Let's show them the limitless possibilities of the childfree lifestyle, and empathy for the grief they're feeling.

Those of you in the military who face rejections including unequal housing, inferior health benefits, inequality of leave, or just being ordered to clean up after an event because you aren't a parent who must run home to your children... speak up! Find others who support your plea for fairness and make it known how you feel. In numbers you may find success and fair treatment.

While traveling, upon checking in at hotels, ask the hotel manager if there is a childfree floor. If not, explain why the hotel may want to consider designating one. It's not because we don't like children; it's because we value our peace and quiet. Kids love to scream, run, and have fun. Vacations are awesome adventures for children. If parents and kids were together on designated floors, they also could enjoy like-minded travelers. The same holds true for airlines and restaurants. Keep requesting childfree areas. You'll often get an eye roll. So what?

If your family is attacking your personal choice to remain childfree and you find yourself thinking, *How dare they come at me with these insane conclusions?* you may want to set them straight. But verbally lashing out at rejection helps neither you nor the rejecter. When people suffer from irrational thinking due to societal brainwashing, they can't see your truths as having merit. If the reality of raising their own children has become a raw disappointment, it's too painful for them to admit it. They can't change *their* life, so they want *you* to undertake the same challenges. They could also be experiencing sheer jealousy of your freedom to choose a childfree lifestyle.

If your family has openly rejected you for not choosing children, find another type of family. Don't remain their victim. I've had many wonder-filled Thanksgivings and other holidays with people I love who accept me for who I am, not what they want me to be. If my own family rejects me, I don't have to accept it. Forget the myth of a family being there for you no matter what. I've said this before and I'll say it again: we're born into families. Sometimes it's not the right fit.

My dear friend Linda Gammon offered this idea: "Instead of trying to get your sister and her family back, simply think of them with love. Send them positive thoughts that they are happy, healthy, and whole. That way, you're not their victim anymore. If they can't see any part of you worth forgiving, what's the loss?" I now practice saying this every night. It's comforting and powerful.

For men who don't want children and haven't considered a vasectomy, think about the ease of your procedure versus that of a woman's. One simply has the "plumbing" fixed. The other faces painful surgery with anesthesia and the possibility of complications in recovery. Also, you'll surely get less rejection from a doctor for your vasectomy request than a woman seeking sterilization would face. Unfair! Sad... but true.

At work, speak up for equality. Remind people that it's not fair to make you take over the duties of a missing co-worker/parent without extra pay. Ask for the same amount of time off given to parents so that you can care for your own ill parents, life partners, family members, or sick animals.

We must acknowledge that people will continue making personal choices that don't reflect our own. Why can't we simply live in peace, allowing for those differences? Do we all need to be reflections of each other? Can you imagine how boring life would be? If someone wants to be a parent, let him or her. Don't attack with disparaging remarks. We don't like that; why would they? They'll never change their minds. We may never change ours, either!

I thought, after a few more insights about feeling pride and not remaining a victim to ignorance or pronatalistic brainwashing, that this would be the end of this chapter. Then I turned on the TV.

Oprah Winfrey was accepting the Cecil B. DeMille Award for lifetime achievement in movies and TV. I was in awe of her impassioned, moving speech. She looked magnificent. Her black wavy hair cascaded around her face. Her large black eyeglasses matched her black dress. The camera showed audience members moved to tears, including her life partner, Stedman Graham, and best friend, Gayle King.

Oprah said, "What I know for sure is, speaking your

truth is the most powerful tool you have!" She didn't say, "Speak to reject! Speak to belittle. Speak to hurt or make anyone feel less than yourselves."

I practiced Oprah's suggestion the very next day. Driving home on a road I've traveled many times, I saw a new assisted-living facility under construction. The sign read, "Inspired Living: We Take Care of Moms and Dads."

Did they mean only parents were going to be admitted? Filled with rage and annoyance at the idea that old people are only moms and dads, I Googled and found the marketing department of this chain of assisted-living properties. I reached a woman who actually listened to me. Not once did I raise my voice while accusing them of selective banishment. I spoke my truth. I spoke my concerns for the many who choose not to parent, can't parent, or shouldn't parent. There was a pause, and then she said, "I'm with you! I've tried pitching what you're saying, but I keep hearing, 'It's our tagline for our brand!'" She suggested I write to her so she could forward the email to the owners. I went one step further: I posted the request on all my Facebook pages. I'm hoping she received more than my one email. However, I still see the same ads.

So, can we come together and accept personal choices without rejecting or being rejected? Maybe. Rhonny's defiant "No!" may also be the truth. We must first accept the fact that there will always be differences of opinion about lifestyle choices and beliefs. The bottom line is, we must love the choices we've made *for ourselves* and love ourselves for those choices.

I know I will continue to face rejection and hear heartbreaking stories of your rejection. As long as I'm on this planet, I'll continue to speak and write to enlighten.

I'll always be open to helping anyone who reaches me through my blog, Instagram, Twitter, Reddit, or numerous Facebook support sites. If I have the pleasure of meeting you in person at a NotMom Summit, a convention, a book signing, a screening of the two documentaries I'm honored to be in, or on one of my NOKID cruises, I'll continue to support and validate you for this choice and work for the equality we deserve.

Want to know the best way to overcome rejection aimed at your childfree lifestyle? Get to know, love, treasure, and feel proud of the possibilities this lifestyle offers. Get to understand the challenges and 24/7 realities of raising children. Spend time with people raising children. Not a few hours. Try a few days, or better yet, a few weeks if possible. Raise your consciousness to the pronatalism that saturates the media, cultural expectations, religions, and expectations from family and friends.

Keep a daily diary of what you did that day. Look at it every night. What was your day like? Of course, there will be conflicts and challenges. All lifestyles face that. Zero in on those moments of peace and contentment, and the opportunities to do what you want when you want to. In other words, start wrapping your hearts around your childfree lifestyle.

Check your life:

1. Do you have definitive short- and long-term goals that offer you wonderful opportunities?

2. Do you have friends who make your heart sing when you're with them? Remember: to get a friend, you have to be a friend. You may have to step out of your comfort zone to find meaningful relationships. You may have to start a

meetup.com in your area. You may have to consider the possibility of moving to a more urban environment.

3. Do you have fun? Are you involved with a hobby or education, dancing alone to music you love, taking piano lessons, singing out loud in the shower or car, or having massages to ease the stresses of being human? Can you plan and save for a vacation you always wanted to experience?

4. Do you reach out to your community and help other humans, animals, or this planet? There's nothing that makes your life richer than knowing your life touched another in a positive way. It's not a gift to them. It's a gift to you.

5. If you feel a nurturing void in your life, there are many organizations in dire need of volunteers. Many children adore those volunteers because, sadly, they don't have a meaningful relationship with any parent or grandparent. There are Boys and Girls Clubs, mentoring programs, Big Brothers Big Sisters, and so many more. I don't have room to list them all here. Google them.

6. If it's not children you want to nurture, but you still feel a nurturing void, try rescuing a pet or volunteering at a senior citizen center or delivering food to aging people with Meals on Wheels. You'll hear anguished stories from older people about how they feel forgotten by their children, and how they appreciate you. It's a good lesson.

7. Read and research on the Internet. When I first started this journey, there was one book about child-freedom, *The Baby Trap*, by Ellen Peck. If she were alive today, she would be shocked, and then, I feel certain, delighted to see how many books there now are on this topic. I never see a new book as competition. It's proof of

the growing need for sources of information worldwide. The more books, articles, YouTube interviews, and documentaries you experience, the better. Check out www.goodreads.com/shelf/show/childfree.

8. Finally, nurture your own inner child. Make sure he or she is happy, fulfilled, contented, safe, and enjoying the opportunities afforded by the childfree lifestyle.

Once you can check off that list in the affirmative and acknowledge the opportunities of the childfree lifestyle, once you acknowledge that you're your own person who knows yourself the best, you'll know how to remedy rejection's effects.

At seventy-six, I do feel wiser than when I was younger. I've fought long and hard for acceptance of the childfree lifestyle as a viable and respectable choice. I've faced rejection and condemnation. Sometimes I still do, even from within the childfree community. At times I've lashed out. At times I've clenched my teeth and walked away, seething with anger. At times I've simply stared, wide-eyed, at the rampant ignorance surrounding a personal choice.

I've come to this conclusion: you can never change another's way of thinking unless they're ready. Most are not. You can only change yourself. Why should we let others define who we are? With that in mind, there may be times you have to let go of toxic energy created by family, friends, and co-workers. There's a peace that comes with letting go.

If enough of you continue on the positive path of speaking your truths while enlightening and teaching, this period of rejection over the childfree lifestyle may be only a brief lesson covered in a future history book.

Acknowledgements

There are many people I want to thank for helping me with this second book. To my husband: what would I have done without your support, constructive criticism, and patience? Hearing me wail, "Shoot me now! I can't do this again!" never stopped you from giving me the courage to finish after three long years. Without your help on this computer, I would have gone insane.

To Dr. Duffy Spencer: the endless hours and commitment you dedicated to the foreword and your professional psychosocial perspective is truly a gift to readers.

To the moderators/administrators of my Facebook sites, Kristin C., Carmen Boone, Jordyn Beranek, Shannon Smigo, Stephanie Watson, John Wimer, Frank Paul Ang, after Nicole Comeau and Kelly Cook: knowing you were monitoring those busy sites day and night when I wanted to write made me feel secure. You settled disputes, threw out trolls, and deleted comments we decided were against our rules. I love you all.

Such a heart-wrenching loss from the sudden passing for me and all who knew my Blair Larae Shields: allowing my posts on your Facebook site "Respectfully Childfree," treating me to brunch at the premiere of the documentary *To Kid or Not To Kid*, patiently teaching me about Instagram, and the light dancing in your eyes when you talk about helping others in the childfree community makes me feel honored and thankful to love you.

To Nicole Comeau: since the time we met, I knew you would be another champion for child-freedom. I also love when you fiercely defend me against the haters. Every time you called, texted, or emailed when you heard an ignorant attack on the Internet reminded me that there are more of you than the haters out there.

To my best friend, Jane Evers, who said, "Of course you can write book two!" Those words helped me forge ahead. Being with me at the NotMom Summit showed others how friendships can be valued even when one has children and the other doesn't. It's called true friendship and unconditional love.

To Helen Jones, who was the first to buy my memoir across the pond, and Samantha Nugent, who traveled from Australia to meet me on a group cruise, and Sarah from the UK and Dani from Brazil: you all touched my life in a special way.

To Carolyn Larson for her amazing talents in proof-reading and her treasured friendship.

To my dog, Pippa: thanks for holding "it" in while I rewrote a paragraph or edited a page!

To all, nationally and internationally, who opened their hearts and communicated honest, sometimes raw feelings: my heart is forever connected to yours. Look how you helped others with what you shared!

A special thank you to Nick Courtright with Atmosphere Press. To anyone who thinks a hybrid publishing company isn't a good choice, they haven't met with Nick and his staff yet. From the moment they accepted this book, I felt enveloped with professional, caring and supported people.

Their wealth of knowledge helped me get you to have this book in your hand or your e-reader. Finally, to my editor, Justine Duhr, and her husband, David, two brilliant teachers of writing, and owners of WriteByNight writers' service (www.writebynight.net): once again, you showed me why editors roam this planet. I'm so fortunate to have you in my life.

To all my followers who write to tell me such wonderful things about being a "pioneer" in the childfree movement: I'm hoping there will be no need for books like this one in the future.

About Atmosphere Press

Atmosphere Press is an independent, full-service publisher for excellent books in all genres and for all audiences. Learn more about what we do at atmospherepress.com.

We encourage you to check out some of Atmosphere's latest releases, which are available at Amazon.com and via order from your local bookstore:

Rags to Rags, nonfiction by Ellie Guzman
The Naked Truth, nonfiction by Harry Trotter
Heat in the Vegas Night, nonfiction by Jerry Reedy
Evelio's Garden, nonfiction by Sandra Shaw Homer
Difficulty Swallowing, essays by Kym Cunningham
A User Guide to the Unconscious Mind, nonfiction by Tatiana Lukyanova
To the Next Step: Your Guide from High School and College to The Real World, nonfiction by Kyle Grappone
Breathing New Life: Finding Happiness after Tragedy, nonfiction by Bunny Leach
Channel: How to be a Clear Channel for Inspiration by Listening, Enjoying, and Trusting Your Intuition, nonfiction by Jessica Ang
Love Your Vibe: Using the Power of Sound to Take Command of Your Life, nonfiction by Matt Omo
Leaving the Ladder: An Ex-Corporate Girl's Guide from the Rat Race to Fulfilment, nonfiction by Lynda Bayada

About the Author

Marcia is an outspoken author and pioneering advocate for parenting choices. Unlike other childfree by choice, she can't be threatened with the possibility she'll change her mind. At 77, that would be impossible. And, she has no regrets.

Her primary focus is on reaching hearts, by dispelling myths and supporting the joys of living a rewarding life without the title of "parent".

In 1974, affected by the shocking consequences of pronatalism, she lost a devoted teaching job after being interviewed on the TV show, "60 Minutes". Facing death threats and picket lines when she spoke, she vowed to overcome the stigma against the childfree lifestyle. At 50, she received her Master's Degree in teaching English as a Second Language. She returned to the profession she loved. In 1998, her peers nominated her for Walt Disney's American Teacher Awards. She retired from teaching in 2000 and now volunteers in a poor community where she teaches ESL.

Marcia was given a Lifetime Achievement Award in 2015 from the Committee for International Childfree Day. Her blog, Facebook sites, childfree group cruises she hosts,

speaking engagements and her books helps understanding that if you want to nurture, there are many ways.
And, if you don't, that's Ok too!

She's interviewed in two documentaries: "To Kid or Not
To Kid" by filmmaker Maxine Trump (No relation) and
"My So-Called Selfish Life" by filmmaker Therese Schecter.

She lives in Florida with her husband Jim and one rescued,
snarky, Chihuahua.

CPSIA information can be obtained
at www.ICGtesting.com
Printed in the USA
BVHW081226210120
570058BV00002B/184